THE CHILDREN'S AID SOCIETY OF NEW YORK

An Index to the Federal, State, and Local Census Records of Its Lodging Houses (1855–1925)

CAROLEE R. INSKEEP

CLEARFIELD

Printed for
Clearfield Company, Inc. by
Genealogical Publishing Co., Inc.
Baltimore, Maryland
1996

Reprinted for
Clearfield Company, Inc. by
Genealogical Publishing Co., Inc.
Baltimore, Maryland
1998, 2000, 2005

International Standard Book Number: 0-8063-4623-X

Made in the United States of America

For my cousin

Sally J. La Grow

who first told me about
The Children's Aid Society

CONTENTS

ACKNOWLEDGMENTS

This book could not have been written without the extensive resources of the U.S. History, Local History & Genealogy Division of The New York Public Library; the Municipal Archives of the City of New York; the National Archives & Records Service (Northeast Region); and the New York Genealogical and Biographical Society. I especially thank my husband, Steve, whose unfailing support made this book possible.

INTRODUCTION

In August of 1917, a young mother abandoned her baby daughter on the steps of the Children's Aid Society at 422 West Twenty-third Street. She left an unsigned note requesting that she someday be allowed to see the child "and kiss her sometimes." Employees took the baby inside and began to search for the mother.

When they failed to find her, the Society contacted the *New York Herald*. The next day, the newspaper printed a photograph of the little girl clutching her doll, along with a notice assuring the mother that she would be allowed to visit her daughter if she would identify herself. The woman materialized within hours. She explained that she worked as a maid and had no one to look after her daughter while she was away from home. While the case was technically one of child abandonment, the Children's Aid Society concluded that the woman simply needed day care for her daughter. It arranged to place the baby in a temporary home until the mother could care for her permanently.

The girl with the doll was just one of thousands of children touched by the Children's Aid Society. Founded to improve the condition of New York City's neglected youth, the Society offered housing, food, clothing, education, and employment to those who needed it most. It provided day care centers and foster home care for children like the little girl left on the doorstep. Of all its early work, the Society is best known for its "Emigration Plan" which removed 30,000 children from New York City's streets to private homes in the country between 1854 and 1929. Many of those sent out were recruited from the Society's lodging houses; this book contains all of the available census records of those facilities.

Before the Children's Aid Society was established in 1853, few groups, public or private, existed to help needy children. The *New York Times* reported that thousands of youngsters had "gained a precarious subsistence for themselves or their parents by pilfering and begging; others swept the crossings; picked over the ash-boxes; gathered rags, bones and refuse paper; others still sold matches, toothpicks, or other small articles, or peddled apples, oranges, and flowers; a large class were newsboys, and print and ballad sellers; others were organ-grinders, statuette sellers, or venders of Bohemian and Dresden ware." Most of them were homeless and slept in boxes or on park benches. Some slept on pavement warmed by newspaper printing vaults during the winter.

It was estimated that three-fourths to four-fifths of New York's vagrant children were the sons and daughters of recent immigrants. The neighborhoods in which they lived profoundly affected a young minister named Charles Loring Brace. He once described the immigrant quarters as "the infamous German 'Rag Pickers Den' in Pitt and Willett Streets, double rows of houses flaunting with dirty banners, and the yards heaped with bones and refuse, where cholera raged unchecked in its previous invasion...murderous blocks in Cherry and Water Streets, where so many dark crimes were continually committed and where the little girls in old shawls who flitted about with baskets became familiar with vice before they were out of childhood." He went on to describe the "vile cellars of the First Ward", "Laurens Street where it was said no drove of animals could pass by and keep its numbers intact", "the community of young garroters and burglars around Hammersly Street", and "the dreadful men and women in 'Poverty Lane' near Sixteenth Street and Ninth Avenue."

Brace believed someone had to help the "young vagabonds and criminals" who lived in these neighborhoods. His propositions to save them have been both admired and criticized throughout the years.

In 1848, New York City's police chief estimated that nearly 10,000 unsupervised, uneducated, and unemployed children roamed the city streets. That year, the Carmine Street Presbyterian Church, of which Brace was a member, established regular "Boys' Meetings," religious services for indigent youths who were reluctant to worship among the affluent. The church made use of songs, pictures, maps, illustrations, anecdotes and simple instruction in an attempt to elevate the boys' education and moral character. The meetings were so successful that nine other groups established similar meetings in other parts of the city. They eventually claimed a total average attendance of over 1,000 boys.

The Boys' Meetings, however, did not provide the children with food or clothing, nor did the meetings take them off the streets for more than a few hours at a time. Wanting to do more, those most active in the original Boys' Meetings organized themselves as the Children's Aid Society in February of 1853. Brace, well traveled and familiar with European social programs, was named Secretary. The group's listing in the 1854 New York City Directory states that "the objects of this society are to help the class of destitute children of New York, by opening Sunday Meetings and Industrial Schools and, gradually, by forming lodging houses and reading rooms for children and by employing paid agents whose sole business shall be to care for them."

If proposed today, the Society's most famous program might spark outrage. In his now infamous essay, The Best Method of Disposing of Our Pauper and Vagrant Children (1859), Brace noted the national demand for child labor. He argued that the Children's Aid Society should:

."..connect the supply of juvenile labor of the city with the demand from the country, and...place unfortunate, destitute, vagrant, and abandoned children at once in good families in the country....We have no hesitation in saying that all the pauper children...young vagrants and petty offenders... might with ease...be placed in good religious homes in our rural districts where every influence exerted upon them would be far healthier and better...."

With this Emigration Plan in mind, the Children's Aid Society approached farmers across the country and invited them to employ vagrant children. The Society agreed to transport the children to the country; in exchange, farmers agreed to provide the children with good homes and work. The first attempt at placement, in 1854, resulted in 300 offers of employment in Michigan. Two-hundred and seven children were successfully placed in "the country."

From the beginning, the Society employed "visitors" to comb through poor neighborhoods. They directed children to the Society's newly formed industrial schools and lodging houses. Others were gathered from local prisons, asylums, and poor houses. Children sometimes presented themselves to the Society in an attempt to escape homelessness, poverty or abuse. Many of them were referred to the Emigration Department.

Children received by the Emigration Department were questioned about their past history, parentage, and physical condition. If accepted into the program, they were bathed and dressed in new clothes. Groups of them were loaded onto trains and sent to towns across the United States. The day after a group arrived, farmers and others desiring to take the children assembled. An advisory committee, composed of "responsible citizens" acquainted with the applicants, located the children primarily in the families of farmers. These children were later dubbed "orphan train riders."

Competing charities organized their own "orphan trains" and "indentured" children to prospective employers. This was a legal arrangement in which the employer agreed to provide for the child "financially and in every other way" as if it were his own . In exchange, the child's labor and good behavior were guaranteed until age eighteen.

The Children's Aid Society did not indenture children to

their employers. Brace regarded this as an advantage, arguing that it was sometimes beneficial to remove a child from an abusive employer or to allow the child to move to a better situation. Brace also believed that an employer would be kinder to the child whose stay was dependent upon affection. Likewise, a child would remain well-behaved if he knew that his continued employment depended upon favorable reviews.

The Society believed that its emigration program was a highly effective way to turn vagrant children into responsible citizens. In its 1928 Annual Report, the Society claimed to have sent 33,000 children to the country. It told the *New York Times* that 87% of the children removed had turned out well, growing up to be "Governors, members of Congress, bankers, merchants, professional men, engineers, and - most conclusive proof - successful farmers."

Proof that the children had actually "turned out well" was hard to come by. The Society had difficulty keeping track of the children once they had been placed in the country. There were accusations that children ran away from their employers or committed crimes. Admitting as much, Brace reasoned that even if one quarter of the children ultimately became a burden to society, the Emigration Plan had not been in vain "for in the city, we can hardly doubt that 95 percent would become in some way burdens to society."

William Letchworth concurred in his report to the 20th National Conference of Charities and Correction in June 1893. He wrote: "Complaints have been made from time to time... against the immigration of such children, some of whom, it was asserted, ran away from their guardians, and became vagrants and criminals. Conceding this to be so... we must conclude that the work of the society has been of incalculable benefit. Had the children... placed in the West been left to roam the streets of New York, the great mass of them would have become vagrants and criminals... they would have infested the Western States as well as the Eastern, and increased the number of the dangerous classes in every State of the Union. By placing these in Western homes, the great majority of them have been made good citizens, to the immeasurable advantage of the country at large."

Brace further argued that the Emigration Plan did not require a high-priced asylum, a large staff, or a burdensome per capita expense. Aside from clothing, which was mostly donated or made by girls in the Society's industrial schools, Brace's organization spent a only a few dollars to transport a child from New York City to a country home. Orphanages that ultimately engaged in similar programs had the same transportation costs, the added expense of supporting the child for a long period of time, large salaries, and high property costs.

In its Annual Report of 1900, the Children's Aid Society noted that of the 22,121 children it had sent to permanent homes in the country, nearly 40% had been recruited from the Society's lodging houses.

The first and most renowned lodging house was the Newsboys' Lodging House, opened on the top floor of *The Sun* newspaper building in 1854. Its purpose was to provide temporary housing for the homeless newsboys who worked in Printing-House Square, a plaza bordered by the offices of New York City's best-known newspapers. These boys were thought to constitute a community by themselves, and were regarded as the hardest and most uncontrollable of all the street children in New York.

Beds were rented to the boys for 6 cents a night, but a condition of admission was that the boy should first take a bath. Supper was available for 4 cents. A free meal and an hour of religious instruction were provided on Sundays. Books and games were available during the week. Classes were offered in the evening for boys who would otherwise have no opportunity to attend school.

The Superintendent of the Newsboys' Lodging House, C.C. Tracey, established a "bank" by constructing a table with holes in the top: each hole connected to a numbered box. A boy could deposit a portion of his daily earnings into the hole with his number on it. The bank was opened at the end of the month and what the boy did not withdraw was deposited into an account in his name at the Sixpenny Savings Bank.

During the first year, 408 boys used the lodging house. Tracey claimed that these boys were cleaner, better behaved, more industrious, and more religious as a result of the Society's intervention. This apparent success led to the establishment of at least twenty other lodging houses over the next 70 years. The majority were dedicated to helping homeless boys, but others were set aside for the use of sick children, abandoned babies, homeless women with children, and homeless girls.

Each lodging house contained an industrial school. Children who used the school began the day with a few Scripture verses and ended the day with a hymn. They received traditional schooling in the morning: basic lessons in geography, language, writing, spelling, colors, and music. In the afternoon, the children studied a light trade. The girls learned sewing or housekeeping while the boys practiced carpentry or box-making. Each child was given a "plain, cheap" dinner and clothed with garments which the girls assisted in making. A paid Matron presided over these schools while upper class women volunteered to help the teachers.

Those children who did not stay at the lodging houses often arrived at school unwashed. In a speech to the teachers in 1868, Brace encouraged the staff to open the windows and air out the rooms as much as possible because of "the bad condition of the atmosphere."

In time, the Society realized that the industrial schools did not prepare city boys for life on the farms where many would soon work. In 1894, the Brace Memorial Farm School was opened at Valhalla in Westchester County, New York, just a few miles outside the city limits. It was thought that the Farm School would weed out those who would do well in the country from those who were "too restless or vicious" to go. Each underwent a physical exam and spent an average of two months training for farm life.

Brace believed the most important lesson the industrial schools could teach was the "Lesson of Labor": orderliness, cleanliness, punctuality, and restraint. Truthfulness and thoroughness were encouraged. Drunkenness was discouraged. Under the teachers' guidance, it was hoped the children would grow up to be respectable domestics, carpenters, or factory workers.

The emigration plan, lodging houses, and industrial schools remained until the end of the 1920s. Children's Aid Society President William Church Osborn was then able to claim: "While there are fewer starving children today than in the past, we still find weary little bodies impoverished through improperly selected and ill-prepared food, neglected teeth and tonsils, insufficient sleep, inadequate housing and lack of activity in the open air and sunshine. The weakening of the home as a factor in the child's life calls for aid directly supplemental to the home during the nine-tenths of his time which he spends outside his school." To address these new problems, the Society reevaluated its work. It closed down the industrial schools, transferred its students to public schools, and converted its old schools into recreational centers. They planned to open a "colored club and health center" in Harlem and a psychiatric clinic for children. They phased out the lodging houses. The Emigration Department became an adoption agency.

The five thousand children named in this index are just a fraction of the people touched by the Children's Aid Society. However, this index includes all those who stayed in a lodging house long enough to be enumerated in a census, making it the largest list yet published. It is hoped that this information will give the descendants of those named, and those who study the history of child care in America, a better understanding of who these children were, what their experiences were, where they came from, and where they hoped to go.

1855

Guide to Column Headings

in the

1855 New York State Enumeration

Name	Name of each person whose usual place of abode was in this institution on the first day of June. Surname first, then the given name and middle initial.
G	Gender. "Female" is designated by "F" and "Male" by "M".
A	Age at last birthday.
Relation	Relationship of each person to the household.
Note	The only lodging house included in this census was the Newsboys' Lodging House at 128 Fulton Street, in the First Election District of the Second Ward. Refer to the original census record for the birthplace, citizenship, and years in New York of each resident.

Name	G	A	Relation
Alty, William	M	15	Lodger
Bulkley, Edward	M	14	Lodger
Clark, George	M	17	Lodger
Coleman, Matthew	M	15	Lodger
Colopy, William	M	32	Lodger
Cross, George	M	15	Lodger
Dailey, John	M	14	Lodger
Davis, William	M	18	Lodger
Kelly, John	M	14	Lodger
Malone, Jamcs	M	18	Lodger
McIntire, Bernard	M	16	Lodger
Moore, Patrick	M	16	Lodger
Nash, Patrick	M	17	Lodger
Nichol, James	M	31	-
Nichol, Jane	F	24	Wife
O'Sulivan, Daniel	M	15	Lodger
Ryan, Richard	M	14	Lodger
Sweeney, Eugene	M	16	Lodger

1860

Guide to Column Headings

in the

1860 Federal Enumeration

Name Name of each person whose usual place of abode was in this institution on the first day of June. Surname first, then the given name and middle initial.

G Gender. "Female" is designated by "F" and "Male" by "M".

A Age at last birthday.

* Notes that information may have been incorrectly reported by the enumerator.

Occupation Work done by each person.

LH Lodging House. The following lodging houses were included in this census:

NWS: Newsboys' Lodging House
128 Fulton Street
Ward 2, Enumeration District 1

RIN: Randall's Island Nursery
Randall's Island
Ward 12, Enumeration District 3

Note — Refer to the original census record for the birthplace of each adult and the birthplace of his or her parents. The enumerator did not make individual entries for children.

Name	G	A	Occupation	LH
Aitken, James H.	M	7	-	RIN
Aitkins, Eliza	F	11	-	RIN
Alcott, Richard	M	9	-	RIN
Alderman, Herman	M	7	-	RIN
Alexander, Sam'l.	M	12	-	RIN
Allen, Edward	M	5	-	RIN
Allen, Symion	M	6	-	RIN
Ambross, Mary E.	F	12	-	RIN
Anderson, Anna	F	4	-	RIN
Anderson, Harriet	F	6	-	RIN
Anderson, Marg't.	F	20	Attendant	RIN
Anderson, Wm. H.	M	12	-	RIN
Anderson, Wm.	M	16	-	RIN
Andrews, Elizabeth	F	35	Attendant	RIN
Appleby, Lunvan	M	16	-	RIN
Arnell, Eugene	M	7	-	RIN
Arnell, John G.	M	9	-	RIN
Arnold, Rob't. H.	M	11	-	RIN
Arnolds, Thos.	M	12	-	RIN
Augustine, J. Wm.	M	10	-	RIN
Augustine, Rob't. H.	M	9	-	RIN
Austin, John	M	8	-	RIN
Babe, Wm.	M	12	-	RIN
Baldwin, Mary	F	49	Attendant	RIN
Barrett, Mary	F	26	Attendant	RIN
Barry, John	M	8	-	RIN
Barry, Richard	M	11	-	RIN
Bash, Fred'k.	M	9	-	RIN
Becket, Mary	F	7	-	RIN
Becks, John	M	4	-	RIN
Bennett, Rob't.	M	11	-	RIN
Bidell, Mary H.	F	11	-	RIN
Biggs, Herman	M	1	-	RIN
Biggs, Wm.	M	5	-	RIN
Bighan, John	M	4	-	RIN
Bigland, James	M	6	-	RIN
Billinger, Emma	F	13	-	RIN
Black, John	M	10	-	RIN
Blanchard, George	M	13	-	RIN

Blasen, Nicholas	M	10	-	RIN
Blimber, Jacob	M	13	-	RIN
Bollands, Biddy	F	44	Attendant	RIN
Bonker, James F.	M	10	-	RIN
Booth, Mich'l.	M	9	-	RIN
Botner, Annette	F	16	-	RIN
Botner, Charlotte	F	13	-	RIN
Botner, Charlotte	F	36	Matron	RIN
Brennan, James	M	8	-	RIN
Brien, Eliza	F	7	-	RIN
Brown, Caroline	F	11	-	RIN
Brown, Charles	M	11	-	RIN
Brown, George	M	7	-	RIN
Brown, James H.	M	8	-	RIN
Brown, Mary	F	9	-	RIN
Brown, Wm.	M	6	-	RIN
Buchman, John	M	5	-	RIN
Buckly, John	M	7	-	RIN
Burk, Chas.	M	8	-	RIN
Burke, Richard	M	10	-	RIN
Burkley, David	M	11	-	RIN
Burns, Elizabeth	F	52	Attendant	RIN
Burns, Francis	M	8	-	RIN
Burns, James	M	11	-	RIN
Burns, John	M	14	Newsboy	NWS
Burns, Wm.	M	8	-	RIN
Butler, Ellen	F	6	-	RIN
Butte, John	M	9	-	RIN
Callahan, Marg't.	F	5	-	RIN
Callahan, Mary	F	9	-	RIN
Callahan, Mary	M*	5	-	RIN
Camp, Mary F.	F	15	-	RIN
Campbell, Archibald	M	7	-	RIN
Carbory, Elizabeth	F	4	-	RIN
Carr, Joshua	M	10	-	RIN
Carr, Wm.	M	12	-	RIN
Carroll, Bernard	M	7	-	RIN
Carroll, George	M	4	-	RIN
Cartall, Henry	M	10	-	RIN
Cook, J. Henry	M	9	-	RIN
Carter, John	M	15	-	RIN

Casey, John	M	4	-	RIN
Casey, May	F	25	Attendant	RIN
Cash, Esward	M	15	-	RIN
Caul, Anthony	M	8	-	RIN
Cauldwell, Jane	F	5	-	RIN
Cauldwell, Jane	F	7	-	RIN
Ceagan, John	M	14	-	RIN
Clark, Frank	M	5	-	RIN
Clark, James	M	5	-	RIN
Clark, John	M	9	-	RIN
Clark, Julia	F	6	-	RIN
Clark, Mary	F	39	Attendant	RIN
Clifford, Mich'l.	M	8	-	RIN
Cobb, Jacob	M	10	-	RIN
Cobet, Mary J.	F	5	-	RIN
Cochran, Wm.	M	9	-	RIN
Coles, Louis	M	13	Newsboy	NWS
Collett, Jos. G.	M	11	-	RIN
Collett, Rob't. F.	M	9	-	RIN
Collins, Chas.	M	6	-	RIN
Collins, John	M	7	-	RIN
Collins, Richard	M	13	-	RIN
Collins, Sarah	F	8	-	RIN
Collins, Thos.	M	3	-	RIN
Dowd, James	M	4	-	RIN
Collis, Mary A.	F	6	-	RIN
Colsen, John	M	15	Newsboy	NWS
Colsen, Robert	M	11	Newsboy	NWS
Colson, Wm.	M	17	Newsboy	NWS
Connelly, Mich'l.	M	10	-	RIN
Connor, Mich'l.	M	4	-	RIN
Connor, Pat'k.	M	5	-	RIN
Connors, John	M	6	-	RIN
Cook, Geo.	M	14	Newsboy	NWS
Cook, James	M	8	-	RIN
Cook, John	M	14	-	RIN
Cook, Pat'k.	M	6	-	RIN
Cooway, Bedelia	F	6	-	RIN
Cornell, Levi L.	M	9	-	RIN
Coughty, Henry	M	17	Newsboy	NWS
Coughty, Leonard	M	15	Newsboy	NWS

Coulter, James	M	6	-	RIN
Creigh, Charlotte	F	13	-	RIN
Croll, Russ. J.	M	10	-	RIN
Crouse, Louisa	F	7	-	RIN
Crowe, Cath.	F	5	-	RIN
Crowe, John	M	15	-	RIN
Cull, John J.	M	10	-	RIN
Cullen, John	M	9	-	RIN
Cully, John	M	11	-	RIN
Cully, Mary	F	10	-	RIN
Cummings, Martin	M	2	-	RIN
Cummings, Sarah A.	F	6	-	RIN
Cummins, Geo.	M	17	Newsboy	NWS
Cunningham, Hary	M	5	-	RIN
Cunningham, Thos.	M	8	-	RIN
Cunningham, Wm.	M	2	-	RIN
Curley, Ann	F	28	Attendant	RIN
Currie, James	M	7	-	RIN
Curry, John	M	7	-	RIN
Clark, David	M	8	-	RIN
Curtin, Kate	F	3	-	RIN
Curtin, Mary A.	F	8	-	RIN
Dacey, Thos.	M	12	-	RIN
Daily, Alex	M	10	-	RIN
Daily, James	M	12	-	RIN
Daily, Lawrence	M	12	-	RIN
Daily, Mich'l.	M	11	-	RIN
Dalis, Mich'l.	M	7	-	RIN
Dalton, Wm. E.	M	12	-	RIN
Daly, Cath.	F	8	-	RIN
Daly, John	M	13	-	RIN
Daly, Mary	F	7	-	RIN
Daly, Sarah	F	38	Attendant	RIN
Dary, Francis	M	10	-	RIN
David, Wm.	M	7	-	RIN
Davis, Wm.	M	8	-	RIN
Dawson, J. Henry	M	10	-	RIN
Dawson, James	M	2	-	RIN
Days, John	M	15	-	RIN
Dearman, Rose	F	5	-	RIN
Dearns, Rob't.	M	9	-	RIN

Delany, Eugene	M	7	-	RIN
Delany, Wm. H.	M	9	-	RIN
Dempsey, Marg't.	F	24	Attendant	RIN
Depe, Ann	F	37	Attendant	RIN
Dercy, Frances	F	13	-	RIN
Desmond, Wm. C.	M	39	Clerk	NWS
Devin, Agnes	F	3	-	RIN
Devine, James	M	8	-	RIN
Dickson, Jackson	M	4	-	RIN
Dillen, Thos.	M	7	-	RIN
Dillon, Wm.	M	9	-	RIN
Doherty, Matilda	F	6	-	RIN
Doherty, Mich'l.	M	8	-	RIN
Doherty, Minnie	F	5	-	RIN
Doherty, Roger	M	10	-	RIN
Doherty, Susan	F	31	Attendant	RIN
Doherty, Wm.	M	5	-	RIN
Dolan, Pat'k.	M	9	-	RIN
Donahue, Pat'k.	M	7	-	RIN
Donaldson, John	M	8	-	RIN
Donnelly, James	M	8	-	RIN
Donnelly, Marg't.	F	8	-	RIN
Donnelly, Mary	F	9	-	RIN
Donnelly, Thos.	M	7	-	RIN
Dooley, Thos.	M	8	-	RIN
Dowd, Francis	M	15	Newsboy	NWS
Dowl, Ann	F	9	-	RIN
Downey, Charles	M	5	-	RIN
Doyle, John	M	6	-	RIN
Dreshey, Wm.	M	14	-	RIN
Duck, John	M	14	-	RIN
Duffey, Bellah	M*	14	-	RIN
Duffey, Hugh	M	10	-	RIN
Duffey, John	M	9	-	RIN
Duffy, Hugh	M	10	-	RIN
Duffy, John	M	7	-	RIN
Duffy, Mary	F	13	-	RIN
Dum, Mich.	M	6	-	RIN
Dumphy, Jos.	M	15	Newsboy	NWS
Duncan, Silas	M	14	-	RIN
Dunn, Lawrence	M	14	-	RIN

Dunn, Mary	F	9	-	RIN
Dunn, Thos.	M	2	-	RIN
Dwyer, Daniel	M	6	-	RIN
Eagan, John	M	11	-	RIN
Edward, Joseph	M	10	-	RIN
Edwards, Joseph	M	10	-	RIN
Ellis, John	M	16	Newsboy	NWS
Elsmore, John	M	5	-	RIN
Fallow, John	M	13	-	RIN
Falter, Eugene	M	13	-	RIN
Farrell, John	M	16	-	RIN
Farrell, Pat'k.	M	6	-	RIN
Farrell, Peter	M	5	-	RIN
Farrell, Thomas	M	4	-	RIN
Farrell, Thos. H.	M	5	-	RIN
Fary, Joseph	M	5	-	RIN
Featherstone, Thos.	M	13	-	RIN
Feely, Patrick	M	13	Newsboy	NWS
Feeny, John	M	6	-	RIN
Feeny, Wm.	M	9	-	RIN
Ferguson, Thos.	M	13	-	RIN
Field, Timothy	M	8	-	RIN
Finnins, Mary	F	11	-	RIN
Fisher, Betsy	F	14	-	RIN
Fisher, James	M	5	-	RIN
Fitzpatrick, James	M	16	-	RIN
Fitzsimmon, Marg't.	F	38	Attendant	RIN
Flaherty, Henry	M	4	-	RIN
Flail, Chas.	M	12	-	RIN
Flannery, Edward	M	13	Newsboy	NWS
Flynn, James	M	9	-	RIN
Flynn, John	M	14	Newsboy	NWS
Flynn, Julia	F	9	-	RIN
Flynn, Michael	M	16	Newsboy	NWS
Foley, Dennis	M	8	-	RIN
Foley, Timothy	M	12	-	RIN
Foote, George	M	16	-	RIN
Forsyth, Mathew	M	14	-	RIN
Fort, Marg't. W.	F	55	Matron	RIN
Fortinan, Wm. P.	M	9	-	RIN
Fowler, Thos.	M	6	-	RIN

Frazier, Sam'l. A.	M	12	-	RIN
French, John	M	5	-	RIN
French, John	M	11	-	RIN
French, Thos.	M	14	-	RIN
Gaffney, Thos.	M	6	-	RIN
Gainor, Wm.	M	9	-	RIN
Gallett, Jos. G.	M	6	-	RIN
Galligher, Mich'l.	M	12	-	RIN
Galvin, Dennis	M	16	Newsboy	NWS
Galvin, John	M	12	Newsboy	NWS
Gannon, John	M	7	-	RIN
Gannon, Wm.	M	9	-	RIN
Gany, Ann	F	48	Attendant	RIN
Gardrue, Wm.	M	12	-	RIN
Garrity, Terry	M	7	-	RIN
Gault, Jane	F	7	-	RIN
Gaynor, Julia	F	40	Attendant	RIN
Gaynor, Mary J.	F	17	Attendant	RIN
Gaynor, Wm.	M	6	-	RIN
Geltagly, Dennis	M	2	-	RIN
Gill, Bridget	F	35	Attendant	RIN
Gillespie, Wm.	M	8	-	RIN
Gillhooly, Pat'k.	M	6	-	RIN
Gilligan, Thos.	M	11	-	RIN
Giome, John	M	7	-	RIN
Gleason, Martin	M	15	Newsboy	NWS
Gleason, Mich'l.	M	6	-	RIN
Glynn, John	M	14	Newsboy	NWS
Glynn, Thos.	M	7	-	RIN
Goodale, Edward	M	15	Newsboy	NWS
Gorhan, Edward H.	M	12	-	RIN
Gorman, Mich'l.	M	5	-	RIN
Graff, Christian	M	9	-	RIN
Gray, Francis	M	9	-	RIN
Gray, J. Henry	M	7	-	RIN
Gray, John	M	9	-	RIN
Gray, Jos.	M	5	-	RIN
Gray, Thos.	M	9	-	RIN
Green, Ellen	F	35	Attendant	RIN
Green, James	M	14	-	RIN
Green, Marg't.	F	9	-	RIN

Gregory, Elizabeth	M*	4	-	RIN
Gregory, James	M	7	-	RIN
Gregory, John	M	8	-	RIN
Gregory, Marg't. A.	F	5	-	RIN
Gregory, Pat'k.	M	2	-	RIN
Hageman, Isaac	M	9	-	RIN
Hagon, Susan	F	6	-	RIN
Haley, James	M	16	-	RIN
Haley, Mary	F	28	Attendant	RIN
Halleshaw, Mich'l.	M	5	-	RIN
Hamburgh, Cornelius	M	7	-	RIN
Hamilton, Alex	M	2	-	RIN
Hamilton, John	M	9	-	RIN
Haney, Mich'l.	M	6	-	RIN
Hann, James H.	M	9	-	RIN
Hanney, John	M	2	-	RIN
Hanson, Eliza	F	6	-	RIN
Hanson, John	M	6	-	RIN
Hapen, John	M	7	-	RIN
Harkey, James	M	9	-	RIN
Harkey, Wm. F.	M	6	-	RIN
Harris, Mich'l.	M	10	-	RIN
Harris, Pat'k.	M	5	-	RIN
Harris, Thos.	M	10	-	RIN
Harris, Thos.	M	13	-	RIN
Harrison, Cath.	F	3	-	RIN
Hart, John	M	7	-	RIN
Hart, Marg't.	F	11	-	RIN
Hartman, Chas.	M	10	-	RIN
Hartman, Herman	M	8	-	RIN
Hatfield, John	M	13	-	RIN
Hawley, Ann	F	6	-	RIN
Hayes, Mary	F	7	-	RIN
Hayman, Henry	M	2	-	RIN
Hays, Marg't.	F	26	Attendant	RIN
Henry, James	M	4	-	RIN
Henry, Thos.	M	15	-	RIN
Herman, John	M	11	-	RIN
Hester, James	M	6	-	RIN
Hester, Thos.	M	12	-	RIN
Heyle, Lorenzo	M	11	-	RIN

Higgens, Mary	F	2	-	RIN
Higgins, Ed	M	9	-	RIN
Higgins, Thos.	M	15	Newsboy	NWS
Hobbs, Bridget	F	24	Attendant	RIN
Hogan, Chas.	M	12	-	RIN
Hogan, John	M	9	-	RIN
Hogan, Mary	F	5	-	RIN
Hogan, Thos.	M	7	-	RIN
Holden, Ann	F	30	Attendant	RIN
Holden, Chas.	M	5	-	RIN
Holden, Fred'k.	M	5	-	RIN
Holden, John	M	3	-	RIN
Holly, John	M	12	-	RIN
Holmes, Rob't.	M	8	-	RIN
Holton, Mary A.	F	12	-	RIN
House, Cath.	F	8	-	RIN
Howard, James	M	10	-	RIN
Howard, Sylvester	M	7	-	RIN
Hoylvan, Christian	F*	11	-	RIN
Hozards, John	M	9	-	RIN
Hubbs, Mary	M*	5	-	RIN
Hudson, Alex	M	7	-	RIN
Hughes, Rose	F	6	-	RIN
Hunt, Peter	M	8	-	RIN
Hunt, Rosa	F	9	-	RIN
Hutchings, Chas.	M	8	-	RIN
Inggens, Susan	F	10	-	RIN
Jackson, Chas.	M	8	-	RIN
Jackson, Mary	F	7	-	RIN
Jackson, Wm.	M	9	-	RIN
Jaques, George	M	12	-	RIN
Jobson, John	M	7	-	RIN
Johnson, Andrew	M	3	-	RIN
Johnson, George	M	5	-	RIN
Johnson, James	M	15	-	RIN
Johnson, John	M	12	-	RIN
Johnson, Mary A.	F	5	-	RIN
Jones, Edward	M	8	-	RIN
Jordon, George	M	8	-	RIN
Judge, Joseph	M	11	-	RIN
Kaegle, August	M	7	-	RIN

Kareh, John	M	11	-	RIN
Kearney, David	M	14	-	RIN
Kearny, Wm.	M	7	-	RIN
Keating, Alex	M	7	-	RIN
Keating, Mary	F	5	-	RIN
Keats, Charles	M	8	-	RIN
Keenan, Chas.	M	6	-	RIN
Kehoe, Laurence	M	14	-	RIN
Kelly, Dennis	M	9	-	RIN
Kelly, Edward J.	M	5	-	RIN
Kelly, Edward	M	3	-	RIN
Kelly, Francis	M	9	-	RIN
Kelly, James H.	M	6	-	RIN
Kelly, John H.	M	6	-	RIN
Kelly, John	M	4	-	RIN
Kelly, John	M	6	-	RIN
Kelly, Martin	M	15	-	RIN
Kennedy, Jane	F	25	Attendant	RIN
Kennedy, Laurence	M	14	-	RIN
Kenny, James	M	2	-	RIN
Kieser, Jacob	M	14	-	RIN
Killahan, Anna	F	7	-	RIN
Killolt, Sarah	F	4	-	RIN
Kimsey, Thomas	M	11	-	RIN
King, John	M	9	-	RIN
Kinny, James	M	5	-	RIN
Kirk, Joseph	M	11	-	RIN
Kohl, Edward	M	9	-	RIN
Laam, Thomas	M	9	-	RIN
Laight, J. Francis	M	7	-	RIN
Lain, John	M	4	-	RIN
Lally, J. R.	M	7	-	RIN
Lally, Mich'l. D.	M	9	-	RIN
Lane, Marg't.	F	22	Attendant	RIN
Lang, Jane	F	9	-	RIN
Laughly, Isaac	M	13	Newsboy	NWS
Leahy, Thos.	M	9	-	RIN
Ledden, Emma	F	15	-	RIN
Lee, Jane	F	65	Matron	RIN
Lee, Mary A.	F	9	-	RIN
Lee, Stewart	M	9	-	RIN

Lewis, Burton	M	14	-	RIN
Lill, Martha W.	F	6	-	RIN
Long, Mag't. A.	F	4	-	RIN
Long, Pat'k.	M	12	-	RIN
Lool, Anna	F	13	-	RIN
Loringwald, Christia	F	?5	Attendant	RIN
Losee, Emma	F	11	-	RIN
Loury, Alfred	M	6	-	RIN
Love, John	M	11	-	RIN
Lucy, Mary	F	20	Domestic	NWS
Lynch, Daniel	M	9	-	RIN
Lynch, John	M	9	-	RIN
Lyons, Patrick	M	13	Newsboy	NWS
Mack, Henry	M	18	-	RIN
Mackey, John A.	M	8	-	RIN
Madden, John	M	16	-	RIN
Magee, John	M	6	-	RIN
Magwends, James	M	3	-	RIN
Maher, Mathew	M	8	-	RIN
Maher, Thos.	M	6	-	RIN
Mahon, Marg't.	F	3	-	RIN
Mahony, Marcus	M	12	-	RIN
Malachy, Hannah	F	7	-	RIN
Mally, John	M	12	-	RIN
Mally, Thos.	M	12	-	RIN
Marion, Mich'l.	M	5	-	RIN
Martin, Ann	F	10	-	RIN
Martin, George	M	7	-	RIN
Martin, Mary J.	F	2	-	RIN
Martin, Matilda	F	12	-	RIN
Martin, Walter	M	6	-	RIN
Mass, Wm.	M	13	-	RIN
Masterson, Pat'k.	M	7	-	RIN
Masterson, Wm.	M	13	-	RIN
Maxwell, Jane	F	8	-	RIN
McArmeny, Pat'k.	M	7	-	RIN
McCaffrey, Ann	F	5	-	RIN
McCaffrey, Mary	F	7	-	RIN
McCaffrey, Richard	M	3	-	RIN
McCain, James H.	M	7	-	RIN
McCain, John	M	5	-	RIN

McCanly, Fanny	F	12	-	RIN
McCanly, John	M	10	-	RIN
McCarty, Wm.	M	9	-	RIN
McCavanagh, Ann	F	37	Attendant	RIN
McCavanagh, Henry	M	5	-	RIN
McComb, John	M	8	-	RIN
McConnell, Frank	M	10	-	RIN
McCormack, Johanna	F	12	-	RIN
McCormack, Wm. J.	M	9	-	RIN
McCortland, Mathew	M	19	-	RIN
McCue, Marg't.	F	13	-	RIN
McDermott, Anid	M	8	-	RIN
McDermott, Wm. J.	M	4	-	RIN
McDevit, Martin	M	9	-	RIN
McDevitt, Dominick	M	13	Newsboy	NWS
McDevitt, Jos.	M	16	Newsboy	NWS
McDonald, Owan	M	12	-	RIN
McDonalds, Ed	M	7	-	RIN
McDonalds, Wm.	M	3	-	RIN
McDonell, Alex	M	10	-	RIN
McDonnell, James	M	8	-	RIN
McDonnelly, Eliza	F	5	-	RIN
McDonnough, James	M	9	-	RIN
McDonnough, John	M	9	-	RIN
McDonnough, John	M	11	-	RIN
McFall, Edward	M	8	-	RIN
McFegan, Carl	M	10	-	RIN
McGannon, Rob't.	M	4	-	RIN
McGee, Elizabeth	F	9	-	RIN
McGee, Mary E.	F	16	-	RIN
McGlen, Mary	F	8	-	RIN
McGrath, P.	M	10	-	RIN
McGray, James	M	11	-	RIN
McGway, Marg't.	F	9	-	RIN
McHarkee, Wm.	M	10	-	RIN
McHarken, Charles	M	12	-	RIN
McInnelly, James	M	6	-	RIN
McIntee, Mich'l.	M	8	-	RIN
McKenna, Cath.	F	6	-	RIN
McKeon, Dennis	M	13	-	RIN
McLain, Mary	F	8	-	RIN

McLoughlin, Edward	M	6	-	RIN
McManus, John	M	9	-	RIN
McManus, Mary A.	F	10	-	RIN
McManus, Pat'k.	M	7	-	RIN
McQuade, Connor	M	11	-	RIN
McQuin, James	M	10	-	RIN
McQuincey, Thos.	M	9	-	RIN
McWilliam, Thos.	M	6	-	RIN
Menahan, Wm.	M	4	-	RIN
Menmerman, Louis	M	13	-	RIN
Miller, Mary H.	F	12	-	RIN
Millins, Thomas	M	10	-	RIN
Minturn, James	M	12	-	RIN
Mitchell, Eliza	F	4	-	RIN
Mitchell, Eliza J.	F	6	-	RIN
Monet, Isabella	F	48	Attandant	RIN
Moore, Wm.	M	7	-	RIN
Moran, Henry	M	3	-	RIN
Morgan, Chas.	M	2	-	RIN
Morgan, Emmeline	F	40	Matron	RIN
Morris, Cath.	F	9	-	RIN
Morris, Wm.	M	16	Newsboy	NWS
Morrisey, James	M	4	-	RIN
Mott, Alex'r.	M	19	Newsboy	NWS
Muldroon, James	M	12	-	RIN
Mulhern, James	M	15	-	RIN
Muller, David	M	14	-	RIN
Murphy, James	M	16	Newsboy	NWS
Murphy, Mich'l.	M	8	-	RIN
Murphy, Morris	M	9	-	RIN
Murray, Ed	M	8	-	RIN
Murray, James	M	6	-	RIN
Murray, James	M	7	-	RIN
Murray, Jeremiah	M	9	-	RIN
Murray, John	M	9	-	RIN
Murray, Mich'l. H.	M	10	-	RIN
Murray, Thos.	M	14	Newsboy	NWS
Myers, Jacob	M	7	-	RIN
Nesbitt, Alex	M	14	-	RIN
Newman, Edward	M	10	-	RIN
Nichols, John	M	10	-	RIN

Niles, Francis	M	14	-	RIN
Nugant, Mary F.	F	6	-	RIN
O'Conner, Chas.	M	41	Superintendant	NWS
O'Conner, Mary	F	23	-	NWS
O'Neil, Jos.	M	15	Newsboy	NWS
O'Brien, Chas.	M	8	-	RIN
O'Brien, Francis	M	6	-	RIN
O'Brien, James	M	10	-	RIN
O'Brien, Thos.	M	13	-	RIN
O'Brien, Timothy	M	8	-	RIN
O'Connell, Dan'l.	M	13	-	RIN
O'Connor, Dennis	M	5	-	RIN
O'Connor, Jeremiah	M	10	-	RIN
O'Connor, Mich'l.	M	6	-	RIN
O'Connor, Richard	M	5	-	RIN
O'Hara, Chat.	F	2	-	RIN
O'Hara, James	M	10	-	RIN
O'Hara, Mich'l.	M	8	-	RIN
O'Hara, Thos.	M	6	-	RIN
O'Hare, Cath.	F	33	Attendant	RIN
O'Hare, Mich'l.	M	7	-	RIN
O'Malley, Chas.	M	14	-	RIN
O'Neil, J. F.	M	12	-	RIN
O'Neil, Rob't.	M	6	-	RIN
Page, Wm. H.	M	10	-	RIN
Palmer, Wm. E.	M	6	-	RIN
Parish, Jacob	M	9	-	RIN
Patterson, Andrew	M	11	-	RIN
Peet, John	M	7	-	RIN
Pelt, William	M	4	-	RIN
Persianna, George	M	10	-	RIN
Persyman, Sarah	F	45	Attendant	RIN
Pettibone, John	M	19	Newsboy	NWS
Phalon, Abigal	F	14	-	RIN
Poulson, Jesse H.	M	12	-	RIN
Powell, Emma	F	5	-	RIN
Price, Bridget	F	14	-	RIN
Price, Francis	M	11	-	RIN
Price, Wm.	M	11	-	RIN
Purcell, Daniel	M	9	-	RIN
Purde, William	M	11	-	RIN

Quin, John	M	14	-	RIN
Quin, Mary A.	F	5	-	RIN
Quin, Mich'l.	M	13	-	RIN
Quinlan, Thos.	M	6	-	RIN
Rafferty, Barny	M	10	-	RIN
Ragan, John	M	6	-	RIN
Raynor, Chas.	M	12	-	RIN
Reed, Mary	F	15	-	RIN
Reynolds, Hugh	M	11	-	RIN
Riley, Bernard	M	8	-	RIN
Riley, George	M	11	-	RIN
Riley, Marg't.	F	5	-	RIN
Riley, Thos	M	4	-	RIN
Rily, John	M	11	-	RIN
Ripley, Rufus	M	50	Overseer	RIN
Roach, John	M	7	-	RIN
Robbins, Wm.	M	9	-	RIN
Roberdon, Seybel	M	9	-	RIN
Robinson, Anna	F	48	Asst. Matron	RIN
Robinson, John	M	12	-	RIN
Rock, Thos.	M	7	-	RIN
Rodney, John	M	3	-	RIN
Roleton, Rob't.	M	7	-	RIN
Ross, Chas. H.	M	8	-	RIN
Russell, Bridget	F	28	Attendant	RIN
Russell, Teressa	F	7	-	RIN
Ryan, Bridget	F	48	Attendant	RIN
Ryan, Catharine	F	3	-	RIN
Ryan, John	M	10	-	RIN
Ryan, Mich.	M	7	-	RIN
Sands, Mich'l.	M	12	-	RIN
Schenburg, Louisa	F	9	-	RIN
Schinbing, Jacob	M	4	-	RIN
Schmidt, George	M	5	-	RIN
Scully, Mich'l.	M	10	-	RIN
See, John	M	13	Newsboy	NWS
Seide, George R.	M	9	-	RIN
Seymour, John	M	14	-	RIN
Shanky, John	M	8	-	RIN
Shaughnesy, Wm.	M	15	Newsboy	NWS
Shaw, Wm.	M	8	-	RIN

Shea, Mary J.	F	8	-	RIN
Sheehan, Michael	M	16	Newsboy	NWS
Sheridan, Chas.	M	16	Newsboy	NWS
Sherriden, Julia	F	3	-	RIN
Shield, Mary A.	F	5	-	RIN
Shield, Thomas H.	M	9	-	RIN
Shilds, Cath.	F	38	Attendant	RIN
Shuttleworth, Sarah	F	5	-	RIN
Simpson, Edmund	M	11	-	RIN
Sinclair, Melvina	F	7	-	RIN
Sisson, John	M	10	-	RIN
Skelly, Mary	F	6	-	RIN
Smith, Anna E.	F	6	-	RIN
Smith, Bernard	M	9	-	RIN
Smith, Chas.	M	16	Newsboy	NWS
Smith, Chas. J.	M	10	-	RIN
Smith, Chas. W.	M	9	-	RIN
Smith, Emily	F	7	-	RIN
Smith, John	M	7	-	RIN
Smith, John	M	11	-	RIN
Solter, Pat'k.	M	8	-	RIN
Sott, Eliza A.	F	4	-	RIN
Speeds, Ellen	F	8	-	RIN
Spread, Thomas	M	11	-	RIN
Stansbury, Rob't.	M	11	-	RIN
Stansby, George	M	9	-	RIN
Stewart, Wm.	M	12	-	RIN
Stockwell, George	M	8	-	RIN
Stolt, Julietta	F	6	-	RIN
Stolt, Mary A.	F	8	-	RIN
Stratten, John	M	9	-	RIN
Strong, L.	F	47	Matron	RIN
Sullivan, David	M	7	-	RIN
Sullivan, Delia	F	4	-	RIN
Sullivan, Mich'l.	M	9	-	RIN
Sullivan, Pat'k.	M	8	-	RIN
Sullivan, Wm. C.	M	4	-	RIN
Tappan, Frank N.	M	12	-	RIN
Thomas, Chas.	M	12	Newsboy	NWS
Thomas, David	M	12	-	RIN
Thomas, Edward	M	9	-	RIN

Thompson, Bridget	F	37	Attendant	RIN
Thornteeds, Emma	F	6	-	RIN
Tierny, Mary A.	F	2	-	RIN
Tolten, Mary J.	F	6	-	RIN
Toomey, Maurice	M	7	-	RIN
Toomy, William	M	9	-	RIN
Towell, Mary A.	F	5	-	RIN
Tracey, Cath.	F	7	-	RIN
Tracey, James	M	9	-	RIN
Trainor, John	M	7	-	RIN
Tracey, John	M	6	-	RIN
Tunnecliff, James	M	6	-	RIN
Tupper, Wm.	M	8	-	RIN
Vandenburg, John	M	6	-	RIN
Vanderbeck, Walter	M	10	-	RIN
Vanderbeck, William	M	12	-	RIN
Wall, Eliza	F	5	-	RIN
Walsh, John	M	8	-	RIN
Walsh, Pat'k.	M	14	-	RIN
Ward, Henry	M	14	-	RIN
Ward, James H.	M	9	-	RIN
Ward, Julia M.	F	11	-	RIN
Washington, George	M	2	-	RIN
Weaber, Chas.	M	9	-	RIN
Welsh, Amelia	F	35	Attendant	RIN
Welsh, Mary A.	F	10	-	RIN
Welsh, Mary	F	14	-	RIN
Wenn, Thos.	M	8	-	RIN
Wesly, Wm. B.	M	9	-	RIN
Whalen, Mary A.	F	8	-	RIN
Whalen, Wm.	M	8	-	RIN
Wheeler, John D.	M	6	-	RIN
White, Wm.	M	15	Newsboy	NWS
Whittak, James	M	12	-	RIN
Wiley, Jane	F	23	Attendant	RIN
Wilkins, Geo.	M	13	Newsboy	NWS
Williamson, Dauson	M	11	-	RIN
Williamson, Wm. J.	M	12	-	RIN
Wilson, John	M	7	-	RIN
Wods, Mary	F	40	Attendant	RIN
Woods, James	M	10	-	RIN

Woods, Thos.	M	10	-	RIN
Worner, Mewa	F	10	-	RIN
Wymbs, Mich'l.	M	7	-	RIN
Young, Hugh M.	M	11	-	RIN
Young, Wm. S.	M	6	-	RIN
Zeiss, Henry	M	11	-	RIN

1870

Guide to Column Headings

in the

1870 Federal Enumeration

Name	Name of each person whose usual place of abode was in this institution in the first of June. Surname first, then the given name and middle initial.
R-G	Race and gender. "White" is designated by "W", "Black" by "B", "Male" by "M" and "Female" by "F".
*	Notes that information may have been incorrectly reported by the enumerator.
A	Age at last birthday.
Occupation	Work done by each person.
LH	Lodging House. The following lodging houses were included in the 1870 census:

18th: Eighteenth Street Lodging House
211 West 18th Street
Ward 16, Election District 15
(second enumeration)

BLK: Girl's Lodging House
125 Bleeker Street
Ward 15, Election District 10
(second enumeration)

NWS: Newsboys' Lodging House
49-51 Park Place
Ward 3, Election District 3
(first enumeration)

Note: Refer to the original census record for the birthplace of each resident.

Name	R-G	A	Occupation	LH
Adams, James	WM	14	Newsboy	NWS
Add, Adelia	-F	20	Nurse	BLK
Allen, Imogene	-F	9	-	BLK
Anderson, Jas.	WM	13	Newsboy	NWS
Anderson, John	WM	17	Newsboy	NWS
Anderson, Joseph	WM	11	Newsboy	NWS
Anderson, Thomas	WM	16	Newsboy	NWS
Andrews, Jane	-F	39	Teacher	BLK
Ash, James	WM	11	Newsboy	NWS
Augustein, John	WM	14	Newsboy	NWS
Austen, John	WM	15	Orphan Boy	NWS
Bacon, James	WM	13	Newsboy	NWS
Bailey, Patrick	WM	15	Newsboy	NWS
Bannen, Jas.	WM	16	Newsboy	NWS
Barker, Thoms.	WM	16	Orphan Boy	NWS
Barlow, William	WM	13	Newsboy	NWS
Barlow, William	WM	16	Newsboy	NWS
Beckwith, Jeanette	-F	25	Seamstress	BLK
Bendy, Joseph	WM	17	Newsboy	NWS
Bolger, Annie	-F	20	Servant	BLK
Boyl, Chrls.	WM	18	Newsboy	NWS
Brady, James	WM	14	Newsboy	NWS
Braxton, Jane	-F	35	Seamstress	BLK
Brennan, Ths.	WM	14	Newsboy	NWS
Brown, Jas.	WM	10	Newsboy	NWS
Brown, Joseph	WM	17	Newsboy	NWS
Brown, Patr'k.	WM	16	Newsboy	NWS
Buel, Andrew	WM	17	Newsboy	NWS
Burty, John H.	WM	14	Newsboy	NWS
Callahan, Thms.	WM	15	Newsboy	NWS
Camerly, Jas.	WM	14	Newsboy	NWS
Canard, Kate	-F	10	-	BLK
Canard, Mary	-F	8	-	BLK
Cassedy, Ths.	WM	15	Newsboy	NWS
Cavanaugh, Chrls	WM	17	Newsboy	NWS
Cavanaugh, Ths.	WM	13	Newsboy	NWS
Clain, Catherine	-F	20	Servant	BLK
Clancy, John	WM	13	Orphan Boy	NWS
Clare, Thomas	WM	11	Newsboy	NWS

Clark, Bridget	-F	12	-	BLK
Cogley, Kate	-F	22	Opr. Sew. Mach.	BLK
Cohen, Edward	WM	14	Newsboy	NWS
Collins, Jas.	WM	13	Orphan Boy	NWS
Concklyn, David	WM	16	Newsboy	NWS
Connelly, John	WM	14	Newsboy	NWS
Connelly, Mich'l.	WM	16	Newsboy	NWS
Conners, James	WM	9	Newsboy	NWS
Connoughton, John	WM	18	Newsboy	NWS
Conroy, John	WM	14	Newsboy	NWS
Conway, Mary	-F	25	Seamstress	BLK
Cooper, Jas.	WM	12	Newsboy	NWS
Cosgrove, Fannie	-F	35	-	BLK
Craig, John	WM	15	Newsboy	NWS
Cristel, Patrick	WM	12	Newsboy	NWS
Crowley, Dan'l.	WM	15	Newsboy	NWS
Cullen, Mich'l.	WM	16	Newsboy	NWS
Cullerty, Jas.	WM	16	Newsboy	NWS
Cunningham, John	WM	13	Newsboy	NWS
Cunningham, Mary	-F	25	-	BLK
Curtis, Charles	WM	17	Newsboy	NWS
Dailey, Delia	-F	24	-	18th
Delvine, Mary	-F	20	Seamstress	BLK
Dior, John	WM	14	Newsboy	NWS
Dogherty, Chrls.	WM	18	Laborer	NWS
Donan, John	WM	14	Newsboy	NWS
Donnelly, Mich'l.	WM	17	Orphan Boy	NWS
Donnelly, Ths.	WM	12	Newsboy	NWS
Dorr, Thomas	WM	16	Newsboy	NWS
Dougherty, Chrls.	WM	9	Newsboy	NWS
Dougherty, Chrls.	WM	17	Newsboy	NWS
Dougherty, Wm. Chrls.	WM	17	Newsboy	NWS
Downey, Thoms.	WM	17	Newsboy	NWS
Doyl, James	WM	12	Newsboy	NWS
Doyle, Bridget	WF	30	Domestic	NWS
Doyle, John	WM	14	Newsboy	NWS
Doyle, Mary	WF	34	Domestic	NWS
Dream, Lizzie	-F	30	Servant	BLK
Driscoll, Cornelius	WM	16	Newsboy	NWS
Dudley, William	WM	12	Newsboy	NWS
Duffie, Margaret	-F	40	-	BLK

Duffie, Mary	-F	40	-	BLK
Duffy, Hugh	WM	21	Laborer	NWS
Duffy, Hughy	WM	17	Newsboy	NWS
Duffy, James	WM	16	Newsboy	NWS
Duner, Ira	WM	12	Newsboy	NWS
Eagan, James	WM	15	Newsboy	NWS
Eckert, Rudolph	WM	18	Newsboy	NWS
Ellert, George	WM	16	Newsboy	NWS
Farrel, Jas.	WM	15	Newsboy	NWS
Ferguson, Margaret	-F	32	Servant	BLK
Ferguson, Sarah	-F	2	-	BLK
Finn, William	WM	17	Newsboy	NWS
Fleming, Frank	WM	16	Newsboy	NWS
Foley, John	WM	14	Newsboy	NWS
Ford, Martin	WM	15	Newsboy	NWS
Fox, George	WM	16	Newsboy	NWS
Frazer, Thomas	-M	8	-	BLK
Freer, William	WM	16	Newsboy	NWS
Fullerton, John	WM	16	Newsboy	NWS
Furham, William	WM	14	Newsboy	NWS
Gallagher, John	WM	16	Newsboy	NWS
Garvey, John	WM	12	Newsboy	NWS
Garvey, Thoms.	WM	12	Newsboy	NWS
Gorman, Martin	WM	14	Newsboy	NWS
Gourley, Ann	-F	8	-	18th
Gourley, Jane	-F	38	Matron	18th
Gourley, John	-M	38	Superintendant	18th
Gourley, Margaret	-F	10	-	18th
Gourley, Mary	-F	1	-	18th
Gourley, Sarah	-F	5	-	18th
Graham, Wm. H.	WM	16	Newsboy	NWS
Grant, Lizzie	-F	15	Servant	BLK
Granthan, Will'm.	WM	15	Newsboy	NWS
Gray, Addie	-F	21	Seamstress	BLK
Halford, Geo.	WM	18	Newsboy	NWS
Halvey, Patr'k.	WM	13	Newsboy	NWS
Hanlan, Thomas	WM	14	Newsboy	NWS
Hanney, Bridget	-F	16	-	BLK
Hannon, Robrt.	WM	14	Newsboy	NWS
Harrison, John	WM	16	Newsboy	NWS
Hawkins, John	WM	16	Newsboy	NWS

Hayden, Mary	-F	16	-	BLK
Hays, Steven	WM	17	Newsboy	NWS
Hemingway, John	WM	18	Newsboy	NWS
Hennesey, John	WM	16	Newsboy	NWS
Hoffman, John	WM	13	Newsboy	NWS
Holland, John	WM	13	Orphan Boy	NWS
Hollins, Alexand.	WM	17	Newsboy	NWS
Holster, Emma	-F	20	-	BLK
Homes, Chrls.	WM	12	Newsboy	NWS
Howard, John	WM	11	Newsboy	NWS
Hughs, Thoms.	WM	16	Newsboy	NWS
Hunt, William	WM	17	Newsboy	NWS
Hunter, Bernard	WM	16	Newsboy	NWS
Irvin, Joseph	WM	16	Newsboy	NWS
Jackson, Sam'l.	WM	18	Newsboy	NWS
Johnson, Chrls.	WM	12	Newsboy	NWS
Jones, James	WM	17	Newsboy	NWS
Jones, Thomas	WM	16	Newsboy	NWS
Jones, William	WM	14	Newsboy	NWS
Keef, John	WM	10	Newsboy	NWS
Kells, John	WM	12	Newsboy	NWS
Kelly, James	WM	17	Newsboy	NWS
Kelly, John	WM	14	Newsboy	NWS
Kelly, John	WM	17	Newsboy	NWS
Kelly, Lawrence	WM	16	Newsboy	NWS
Kelly, Patrick	WM	16	Newsboy	NWS
Kelly, Thomas	WM	16	Newsboy	NWS
Kelly, Thoms.	WM	17	Newsboy	NWS
Kennedy, Ann	WF	26	Domestic	NWS
Kerrigan, John	WM	12	Orphan Boy	NWS
Kerry, John	WM	14	Newsboy	NWS
Kills, John	WM	12	Orphan Boy	NWS
Kuhl, Florene	WM	18	Newsboy	NWS
Laden, William	WM	14	Newsboy	NWS
Laight, John	WM	18	Newsboy	NWS
Lanahan, Ths.	WM	17	Newsboy	NWS
Lawler, Annie	-F	26	-	BLK
Linch, Dan'l.	WM	14	Newsboy	NWS
Linch, John	WM	16	Newsboy	NWS
Linch, Thomas	WM	17	Newsboy	NWS
Loenecker, George	-M	30	-	18th

Long, Thomas	WM	12	Newsboy	NWS
Longhworth, Ths.	WM	14	Newsboy	NWS
Lyons, John	WM	14	Newsboy	NWS
Mack, Chrls.	WM	10	Orphan Boy	NWS
Mack, John	WM	16	Newsboy	NWS
Maloney, Edward	WM	12	Newsboy	NWS
Maloney, James	WM	17	Newsboy	NWS
Martin, Edw'd.	WM	13	Newsboy	NWS
Mason, James	WM	17	Newsboy	NWS
McCarthy, John	WM	16	Newsboy	NWS
McClue, Edw.	WM	16	Orphan Boy	NWS
McCluskey, Robr't.	WM	10	Newsboy	NWS
McCue, Edw'd.	WM	16	Newsboy	NWS
McDevitt, Barry	WM	15	Newsboy	NWS
McDevitt, Dmk.	WM	18	Newsboy	NWS
McDonald, Ann	-F	22	-	BLK
McDonald, Fra.	WM	14	Newsboy	NWS
McDonald, John	WM	14	Newsboy	NWS
McDonald, Owen	WM	13	Newsboy	NWS
McGarvin, Thomas	WM	16	Newsboy	NWS
McGinness, Ths.	WM	16	Newsboy	NWS
McGrath, Ann	WF	25	Domestic	NWS
McGrath, Bridget	WF	22	Domestic	NWS
McHenry, John	WM	14	Newsboy	NWS
McKennen, James	WM	16	Newsboy	NWS
McKisick, Emma	-F	24	Housekeeper	BLK
Meiers, John	WM	10	Newsboy	NWS
Mullen, Maggie	-F	16	Nurse	BLK
Murphy, Ann	-F	20	Servant	BLK
Murphy, Ann	-F	33	Servant	BLK
Murphy, Chrls.	WM	14	Newsboy	NWS
Murphy, James	WM	14	Newsboy	NWS
Murphy, James	WM	17	Newsboy	NWS
Murphy, John	WM	17	Newsboy	NWS
Murphy, Robert	-M	17	-	18th
Nack, John	WM	17	Newsboy	NWS
Nack, William	WM	10	Newsboy	NWS
Nash, Felix	WM	14	Newsboy	NWS
Nearey, Cornelius	WM	16	Newsboy	NWS
Nesbit, James	WM	15	Newsboy	NWS
Nesbit, John H.	WM	11	Newsboy	NWS

Newman, William	WM	12	Newsboy	NWS
Night, Edward	WM	11	Newsboy	NWS
O'Brien, John	WM	11	Newsboy	NWS
O'Brien, John	WM	15	Newsboy	NWS
O'Connell, Will	WM	16	Newsboy	NWS
O'Conner, Chrls.	WM	16	Newsboy	NWS
O'Connor, Allice	WF	6	-	NWS
O'Connor, Chrls.	WM	42	Superintendant	NWS
O'Connor, Fred'k.	WM	4	-	NWS
O'Connor, Mary	WF	36	Keeping House	NWS
O'Connor, Pauline	WF	2	-	NWS
O'Donnell, Domnk.	WM	18	Newsboy	NWS
O'Hearn, Kate	-F	6	-	BLK
Parker, Willie	WM	17	Newsboy	NWS
Pendegrast, Will.	WM	11	Newsboy	NWS
Pomroy, John	WM	15	Newsboy	NWS
Price, John	WM	16	Newsboy	NWS
Purtell, Mary	-F	24	-	BLK
Reed, William	WM	17	Newsboy	NWS
Reily, John	WM	14	Newsboy	NWS
Robinson, Frank	WM	16	Newsboy	NWS
Rodey, Mich'l. G.	WM	16	Newsboy	NWS
Ruce, Henry	WM	16	Newsboy	NWS
Ryan, Sarah	-F	30	Servant	BLK
Ryan, Thomas	WM	18	Newsboy	NWS
Scanlon, James	WM	16	Newsboy	NWS
Scanlon, John	WM	12	Newsboy	NWS
Schort, James	WM	17	Newsboy	NWS
Schwan, Mary	-F	12	-	BLK
Shannon, Anna	-F	25	Tailoress	BLK
Shields, John	WM	16	Newsboy	NWS
Simpson, Peter	WM	16	Newsboy	NWS
Skelly, Matthew	WM	15	Newsboy	NWS
Skelly, William	WM	13	Newsboy	NWS
Small, James	WM	17	Orphan Boy	NWS
Smith, James	-M	31	Seamstress	BLK
Smith, John	BM	17	Laborer	NWS
Smith, Nellie	-F	1	-	BLK
Smith, Sarah	-F	20	Servant	BLK
Smith, Thoms.	WM	16	Newsboy	NWS
Smith, William	WM	16	Newsboy	NWS

Stanton, John	WM	17	Orphan Boy	NWS
Sullivan, Chrls.	WM	14	Newsboy	NWS
Sullivan, Dennis	WM	14	Newsboy	NWS
Sullivan, John B.	WM	15	Newsboy	NWS
Sullivan, Lawrence	WM	17	Orphan Boy	NWS
Sullivan, Mich'l	WM	16	Orphan Boy	NWS
Sweeney, John	WM	14	Newsboy	NWS
Terry, John	WM	15	Newsboy	NWS
Thomas, Emma	-F	6	-	BLK
Thomas, Lizzie	-F	8	-	BLK
Thompson, Mary	-F	40	Seamstress	BLK
Thompson, Thmms.	WM	15	Newsboy	NWS
Torolough, Will'm.	WM	11	Newsboy	NWS
Tracey, Garrett	WM	16	Newsboy	NWS
Trot, Cyrus	-M	3	-	BLK
Trot, Eli	-M	38	Superintendant	BLK
Trot, Eloise	-F	6	-	BLK
Trot, Lois	-F	42	-	BLK
Tucker, Robert	WM	15	Newsboy	NWS
Tucker, Thomas	WM	12	Newsboy	NWS
Tuthill, Mary	-F	20	Servant	BLK
VanWinke, Anna	-F	23	-	18th
Vinier, Ellen	-F	30	-	BLK
Wards, Daniel	WM	15	Newsboy	NWS
Wayne, Hannah	-F	17	Nurse	BLK
Wehlan, Ths.	WM	11	Newsboy	NWS
Wehman, John	WM	16	Newsboy	NWS
Wells, Chrls.	WM	16	Newsboy	NWS
Welsh, James	WM	17	Newsboy	NWS
Wiggly, William	WM	16	Newsboy	NWS
Williams, Steen	WM	13	Orphan Boy	NWS
Wilson, Geo.	WM	17	Newsboy	NWS
Yobert, John	WM	16	Newsboy	NWS

1880

Guide to Column Headings

in the

1880 Federal Enumeration

Name Name of each person whose usual place of abode was in this institution on the first of June. Surname first, then the given name and middle initial.

R-G Race and gender. "White" is designated by "W", "Black" by "B", and "Mulatto" by "Mu". Males are designated by "M" and females are by "F".

* Notes that the enumerator may have given incorrect information.

A Age at last birthday. Designated in years, unless otherwise noted with an "m" for "months".

Relation Relationship of each person to the institution.

LH Lodging House. The following lodging houses were included in this census:

11th: Eleventh Ward Lodging House
709 East 11th Street
Assembly District 14
Enumeration District 376

18th: Eighteenth Street Lodging House
211 West 18th Street
Assembly District 13
Enumeration District 334

35th: Thirty-fifth Street Lodging House
314 East 35th Street
Assembly District 18
Enumeration District 491

NWS: Newsboys' Lodging House
9 Duane Street
Assembly District 2
Enumeration District 36

RIV: Rivington Street Lodging House
327 Rivington Street
Assembly District 6
Enumeration District 133

SMP: Girls' Lodging House
27 St. Mark's Place
Assembly District 14
Enumeration District 355

Note Refer to the orginal census for the birthplace of each person and his or her parents.

Name	R-G	A	Relation	LH
Adam, Henry	WM	17	Lodger	18th
Adams, Charles	WM	16	Lodger	RIV
Adams, Fredaerick	WM	18	Lodger	RIV
Allen, William	WM	18	Lodger	RIV
Antwine, Jacob	BM	16	Boarder	NWS
Bachelor, Mary	WF	52	Housekeeper	SMP
Backinan, Joseph	WM	15	Boarder	NWS
Bannon, James	WM	17	Boarder	NWS
Bannon, Thomas	WM	17	Boarder	35th
Barrett, Sarah	WF	20	Boarder	18th
Barry, William	WM	16	Lodger	RIV
Baur, Bernard	WM	17	Lodger	18th
Bell, Jennie	WF	3	Lodger	SMP
Bench, James	WM	17	Lodger	18th
Benn, William	WM	16	Lodger	18th
Benney, Charles	WM	17	Lodger	11th
Bethel, John	WM	18	Lodger	18th
Blake, Adam	WM	18	Lodger	18th
Blake, George	WM	16	Lodger	RIV
Boos, Frederick	WM	17	Lodger	18th
Borden, James	WM	22	Lodger	11th
Boscher, Jos. C.	WM	3	Boarder	11th
Boyle, Thomas	WM	17	Boarder	NWS
Brady, George	WM	16	Lodger	18th
Brady, John	WM	14	Boarder	35th
Brady, John	WM	16	Boarder	35th
Brady, Wm.	WM	15	Boarder	35th
Brennan, Joseph	WM	17	Boarder	NWS
Brewell, Charles	WM	14	Boarder	35th
Brown, Charles	WM	16	Lodger	11th
Brown, Clara	WF	8	Lodger	SMP
Brown, Edmond	WM	16	Son	11th
Brown, Elizabeth	WF	25	Daughter	11th
Brown, Isabella	WF	21	Daughter	11th
Brown, Mararet E.	WF	48	Matron	11th
Brown, Thomas	WM	17	Lodger	RIV
Brush, Philip	WM	16	Lodger	RIV
Burke, Francis	WM	22	Employee	RIV
Burke, James	WM	16	Boarder	35th

Burke, John	WM	14	Boarder	35th
Burke, Laurence	WM	12	Lodger	18th
Burke, Walter	WM	15	Boarder	35th
Burke, William	WM	16	Lodger	18th
Butcher, Harry	WM	18	Lodger	11th
Cahill, Hanna	WF	20	Servant	NWS
Calcutt, William	WM	14	Boarder	NWS
Callaghan, James	WM	12	Lodger	RIV
Callaghan, John	WM	16	Boarder	NWS
Callaghan, Mich'l.	WM	14	Lodger	RIV
Callahan, Dan'l.	WM	17	Boarder	35th
Callahan, Edwd.	WM	17	Boarder	35th
Callan, John	WM	17	Boarder	35th
Campbell, James	WM	14	Boarder	35th
Carel, Theodore	WM	15	Boarder	NWS
Carl, Isidore	WM	15	Boarder	NWS
Carr, James	WM	17	Lodger	18th
Carraher, John	WM	17	Lodger	RIV
Carroll, John	WM	15	Lodger	RIV
Carson, William	WM	17	Boarder	35th
Casey, James	WM	16	Lodger	RIV
Casey, Joseph	WM	13	Lodger	RIV
Cassidy, Henry	WM	12	Lodger	RIV
Cavanagh, James	WM	13	Boarder	NWS
Cavanagh, John	WM	14	Lodger	18th
Cavanagh, Mary	WF	8	Lodger	SMP
Clancy, Mary	WF	3	Lodger	SMP
Clarissa, George	WM	20	Lodger	11th
Clark, Annie	WF	10	Lodger	SMP
Clark, Minnie	WF	6	Lodger	SMP
Clement, William	WM	15	Lodger	18th
Cohen, Harris	WM	16	Boarder	NWS
Cohen, Seinon	WM	16	Boarder	NWS
Collins, Daniel	WM	16	Boarder	35th
Collins, James	WM	14	Boarder	35th
Collins, John	WM	19	Boarder	NWS
Condit, Fletcher	WM	18	Lodger	18th
Conlin, James	WM	20	Lodger	11th
Conly, Thomas	WM	17	Lodger	18th
Conly, William	WM	16	Lodger	18th
Conmarty, Thomas	WM	17	Boarder	35th

Connolly, Kate	WF	16	Servant	NWS
Connolly, Stephen	WM	14	Boarder	NWS
Consoldt, Elizabeth	WF	12	Lodger	SMP
Conway, John	WM	17	Boarder	NWS
Cooper, Thomas	WM	12	Boarder	NWS
Corbett, James	WM	16	Boarder	35th
Corcorren, Charles	WM	16	Boarder	NWS
Corner, Edward	WM	19	Lodger	11th
Corr, Robert	WM	17	Boarder	35th
Cosbin, Nathan	WM	19	Lodger	11th
Coyne, Abraham	WM	15	Lodger	RIV
Crane, William	WM	12	Lodger	RIV
Crawfort, Samuel	WM	13	Lodger	RIV
Crosby, Robert	WM	12	Lodger	RIV
Crow, William	WM	15	Boarder	35th
Crowley, Jeremiah	WM	18	Boarder	35th
Cummins, Benj.	WM	15	Boarder	35th
Cunningham, George	WM	17	Lodger	11th
Cunningham, Robert	WM	18	Lodger	11th
Cupps, Delia	WF	8	Lodger	SMP
Curran, James	WM	16	Boarder	35th
Curry, Frank	WM	16	Boarder	35th
Cutter, Fannie	WF	9	Lodger	SMP
Daly, James	WM	15	Boarder	35th
Daly, Michael	WM	15	Boarder	NWS
Degraw, Henry	WM	16	Boarder	NWS
Denton, Charles	WM	17	Boarder	35th
Devlin, John	WM	15	Lodger	RIV
Dillon, William	WM	18	Lodger	18th
Dizerens, Emille	WM	18	Lodger	18th
Dolan, Edmond	WM	17	Lodger	11th
Dolan, James A.	WM	14	Boarder	NWS
Donay, John	WM	15	Lodger	RIV
Donnelly, Annie	WF	10	Lodger	SMP
Donnelly, Joseph	WM	17	Boarder	35th
Donohue, Joseph	WM	17	Boarder	NWS
Donovan, James	WM	23	Lodger	11th
Donovan, John	WM	15	Boarder	NWS
Doran, Patrick	WM	14	Boarder	35th
Down, Mary	WF	38	Housekeeper	SMP
Doyle, James	WM	17	Boarder	35th

Drew, Emma	WF	11	Lodger	SMP
Drone, Annie	WF	8	Lodger	SMP
Duffy, Laurence	WM	18	Lodger	RIV
Eames, Nellie	WF	56	Teacher	SMP
Edwards, Michael	WM	13	Lodger	RIV
Egan, Hubert	WM	12	Lodger	RIV
Egglestone, Jno.	WM	16	Boarder	35th
Eichert, Morris	WM	14	Boarder	NWS
Eiden, Fred'k.	WM	17	Boarder	35th
Eiling, John	WM	16	Boarder	35th
Elatie, Ernest	WM	16	Boarder	NWS
Ellenon, Moses	WM	13	Lodger	11th
Elliott, James	WM	16	Lodger	18th
Enfield, Louis	WM	14	Boarder	NWS
English, Thomas	WM	19	Boarder	35th
Evan, John	WM	18	Lodger	11th
Fannin, Michael	WM	19	Lodger	11th
Farley, Thomas	WM	15	Boarder	35th
Farnell, James	WM	12	Boarder	NWS
Farrel, Thomas	WM	13	Boarder	NWS
Farrell, William	WM	16	Boarder	35th
Farrington, Denis	WM	18	Boarder	35th
Fasting, John	WM	17	Lodger	11th
Flannagan, Christie	WM	10	Lodger	18th
Fletcher, William	WM	20	Lodger	11th
Flood, Henry	WM	15	Boarder	35th
Flynn, Patrick	WM	18	Lodger	18th
Flynn, Peter	WM	15	Boarder	35th
Foley, Michael	WM	17	Boarder	NWS
Ford, Daniel	WM	16	Lodger	18th
Ford, James	WM	19	Lodger	11th
Forrey, Lena	WF	19	Servant	35th
Foster, John	WM	16	Lodger	RIV
Furguson, James	WM	17	Lodger	11th
Gabriel, Martin	WM	21	Lodger	11th
Gainer, Thomas	WM	15	Boarder	NWS
Gaines, John	WM	16	Boarder	NWS
Gallagher, Patrick	WM	16	Boarder	NWS
Galloway, Fredrick	WM	13	Boarder	NWS
Gavin, William	WM	19	Lodger	11th
Geilerges, Maynes	WM	20	Lodger	11th

Gilbert, James	WM	17	Lodger	11th
Gilbert, Thomas	WM	15	Lodger	RIV
Gilkewson, John	WM	16	Lodger	11th
Gilligan, James P.	WM	16	Boarder	NWS
Gottschaer, William	WM	15	Lodger	18th
Grady, John	WM	14	Boarder	NWS
Gray, John	WM	17	Boarder	NWS
Grennon, John	WM	14	Boarder	35th
Guilday, Patrick	WM	14	Boarder	NWS
Hall, James	WM	18	Lodger	18th
Hardy, John	WM	18	Lodger	11th
Harrington, John	WM	19	Boarder	NWS
Harrison, John	WM	18	Boarder	NWS
Hart, John	WM	17	Boarder	NWS
Heincke, Charles	WM	20	Servant	NWS
Henry, John	WM	18	Lodger	RIV
Hickey, Thomas	WM	17	Boarder	35th
Higgins, David	WM	19	Lodger	11th
Hitgannon, James	WM	15	Lodger	18th
Hogan, James	WM	12	Lodger	RIV
Hogan, Michael	WM	16	Boarder	35th
Holland, William	WM	18	Boarder	NWS
Holt, Robert	WM	17	Boarder	35th
Hunt, Fred'k.	WM	17	Lodger	18th
Hunter, Rich.	WM	16	Lodger	RIV
Hurley, Elizabeth	WF	45	Matron	SMP
Hydt, George	WM	17	Lodger	18th
Isaac, Joseph	WM	15	Boarder	NWS
Isaacs, Jacob	WM	17	Boarder	NWS
Jackson, James	WM	18	Lodger	18th
Jackson, John	WM	19	Lodger	18th
Johnson, John	WM	18	Boarder	NWS
Johnson, William	WM	16	Lodger	18th
Johnson, William	WM	18	Lodger	18th
Jones, Barclay	WM	18	Lodger	RIV
Jones, Robert	WM	14	Boarder	NWS
Jones, Thomas	WM	12	Boarder	NWS
Jordon, William	WM	16	Boarder	35th
Joyce, John	WM	16	Lodger	RIV
Kane, John	WM	23	Lodger	11th
Kaulmire, Chas.	WM	16	Boarder	35th

Kearney, Owen	WM	16	Lodger	RIV
Kelly, David	WM	12	Lodger	11th
Kelly, James	WM	16	Lodger	RIV
Kelly, James	WM	18	Lodger	11th
Kelly, John	WM	13	Lodger	RIV
Kelly, John	WM	16	Boarder	NWS
Kelly, Joseph	WM	14	Boarder	35th
Kelly, Michael	WM	15	Lodger	RIV
Kelly, William	WM	15	Lodger	RIV
Kempton, David	WM	15	Lodger	11th
Kempton, Robert	WM	17	Lodger	11th
Kempton, Samuel	WM	13	Lodger	11th
Kenny, James	WM	20	Boarder	NWS
Kenyon, Charles	WM	16	Boarder	NWS
Kerrigan, John	WM	13	Lodger	RIV
King, William	WM	14	Lodger	18th
Kranes, John	WM	18	Boarder	35th
Lariety, Pat'k.	WM	12	Boarder	35th
Laurence, Joseph	WM	15	Lodger	RIV
Lawson, John	WM	16	Lodger	11th
Leamen, Lizzie	WF	6	Lodger	SMP
Lee, Charles	MuM	16	Boarder	NWS
Lee, James	WM	16	Boarder	NWS
Lennon, John	WM	16	Boarder	35th
Lennon, Thomas	WM	16	Boarder	35th
Leonard, Frank	WM	16	Lodger	RIV
Lingley, Mary	WF	8	Lodger	SMP
Linyard, Patrick	WM	16	Boarder	NWS
Long, Edward	WM	16	Boarder	NWS
Luttrell, James	WM	17	Lodger	11th
Lynch, Bernard	WM	15	Boarder	35th
Lynch, Bridget	WF	17	Servant	NWS
Lynch, Frank	WM	18	Lodger	18th
Lynch, John	WM	18	Lodger	RIV
Lynch, Thomas	WM	14	Boarder	NWS
Lyons, Annie	WF	7	Lodger	SMP
Macabe, Owen	WM	17	Lodger	11th
Mack, Thomas	WM	16	Boarder	35th
Madden, James	WM	16	Lodger	RIV
Maherdell, Joseph	WM	8	Lodger	18th
Maherdell, Patrick	WM	12	Lodger	18th

Malloch, William	WM	16	Boarder	NWS
Maroney, John	WM	17	Boarder	NWS
Martin, George	WM	18	Lodger	RIV
Martin, James A.	WM	16	Boarder	NWS
Martin, John	WM	17	Boarder	NWS
Matchern, Emma	WF	30	Wife	35th
Matchern, Harry	WM	37	Superintendant	35th
May, John	WM	17	Lodger	RIV
McAlp-e, Mary	WF	37	-	SMP
Mcarthy, William	WM	17	Boarder	NWS
McCane, John	WM	18	Lodger	11th
McCarter, Ann	WF	11	Daughter	35th
McCarter, Ann	WF	45	Housekeeper	35th
McCarthy, John	WM	21	Boarder	NWS
McCormack, John	WM	16	Boarder	35th
McCormack, Mich.	WM	15	Boarder	35th
McCormack, Thomas	WM	14	Boarder	35th
McCully, Hannah	WF	26	Wife	18th
McCully, William	WM	11m	Son	18th
McCully, William	WM	34	Husband	18th
McCune, Mary	WF	8	Lodger	SMP
McDonald, Andrew	WM	12	Lodger	18th
McDonald, Edward	WM	16	Boarder	NWS
McGlinchy, Ellen	WF	12	Lodger	SMP
McGough, John	WM	18	Boarder	35th
McGough, Mich'l.	WM	15	Boarder	35th
McGough, Terence	WM	17	Boarder	35th
McGovern, Lawrence	WM	17	Boarder	35th
McGrath, Bridget	WF	30	Servant	NWS
McGuinness, William	WM	16	Lodger	11th
McGuire, John	WM	14	Boarder	35th
McGuire, William	WM	15	Boarder	35th
McKay, Robert	WM	13	Boarder	NWS
McKenna, James	WM	15	Lodger	11th
McKernan, William	WM	17	Boarder	NWS
McLaughlin, Wm.	WM	16	Boarder	35th
McLoughlin, Mich'l.	WM	16	Lodger	18th
McManus, Alec	WM	16	Boarder	35th
McNally, Michael	WM	17	Lodger	18th
McNeil, Charles	WM	11	Boarder	NWS
McNully, James	WM	14	Lodger	11th

McSean, James	WM	19	Lodger	11th
McShane, George	WM	16	Boarder	NWS
Meehan, Thomas	WM	28	Boarder	11th
Mende, Henry	WM	17	Lodger	RIV
Miller, Edward	WM	15	Lodger	18th
Miller, John	WM	17	Lodger	RIV
Monaghan, James	WM	17	Boarder	35th
Moore, John	WM	16	Lodger	18th
Moore, John	WM	24	Lodger	11th
Moore, Michael	WM	20	Lodger	11th
Morgan, William	WM	15	Boarder	NWS
Morrell, Elizabeth	WF	7	Lodger	SMP
Morrell, Jno.	WM	16	Boarder	35th
Morris, Fred'k.	WM	18	Boarder	35th
Morrow, Mary	WF	7	Lodger	SMP
Morton, James	WM	17	Lodger	11th
Mulcahy, Timothy	WM	17	Boarder	NWS
Mullady, Michael	WM	17	Boarder	35th
Mulligan, James	WM	18	Lodger	18th
Mulligan, Owen	WM	17	Lodger	18th
Murphy, John	WM	11	Lodger	RIV
Murphy, John	WM	18	Lodger	RIV
Murphy, Michael	WM	18	Lodger	18th
Murphy, William	WM	14	Boarder	NWS
Murphy, William	WM	18	Boarder	35th
Murray, James	WM	16	Boarder	NWS
Murray, John	WM	18	Lodger	RIV
Murray, Peter	WM	18	Boarder	35th
Murray, Wm.	WM	16	Lodger	RIV
Myers, James	WM	11	Lodger	RIV
Nanlon, William	WM	15	Boarder	35th
Nathan, Abraham	WM	16	Lodger	RIV
Nevins, James	WM	18	Lodger	11th
Nolan, Wm. H.	WM	18	Lodger	RIV
Nugent, Daniel	WM	15	Lodger	18th
Nurley, Jno.	WM	16	Boarder	35th
O'Brien, James	WM	10	Lodger	RIV
O'Brien, Jno.	WM	15	Boarder	35th
O'Brien, John	WM	15	Boarder	NWS
O'Brien, John	WM	18	Lodger	18th
O'Brien, Peter	WM	16	Boarder	35th

O'Brien, Thomas	WM	15	Boarder	35th
O'Connor, Alice	WF	14	Daughter	NWS
O'Connor, Charles	WM	8	Son	NWS
O'Connor, Charles	WM	54	Superintendant	NWS
OConnor, Fredrick	WM	15	Son	NWS
O'Connor, Mary	WF	45	Matron	NWS
O'Connor, Pauline	WF	11	Daughter	NWS
O'Hare, Edwd.	WM	18	Boarder	35th
O'Shea, Mortimer	WM	14	Boarder	NWS
Parker, Thomas	WM	16	Boarder	NWS
Paye, Lottie	WF	10	Lodger	SMP
Phelan, William	WM	21	-	RIV
Pierce, James	WM	16	Boarder	35th
Pinckney, Conselyea	WM	17	Son	SMP
Pollock, William	WM	23	Boarder	18th
Post, William	WM	13	Boarder	35th
Putnam, Stephen	WM	65	Lodger	SMP
Quinn, Joseph	WM	17	Boarder	35th
Quinn, Peter	WM	17	Boarder	35th
Quinn, Richard	WM	17	Boarder	35th
Regan, Andrew	WM	16	Boarder	NWS
Regan, Edward	WM	18	Lodger	18th
Regan, James	WM	13	Lodger	11th
Regan, Thomas	WM	22	Lodger	11th
Reilly, Frank	WM	17	Boarder	NWS
Reilly, George	WM	14	Boarder	35th
Reilly, James	WM	15	Lodger	RIV
Reilly, James	WM	17	Boarder	35th
Reilly, Michael	WM	17	Boarder	NWS
Reynolds, William	WM	16	Boarder	NWS
Rice, James	WM	14	Boarder	NWS
Rice, Phillip	WM	15	Boarder	NWS
Ried, David	WM	13	Boarder	35th
Ried, George	WM	14	Boarder	35th
Riley, James	WM	16	Boarder	NWS
Riley, Thomas	WM	17	Lodger	11th
Robar, Charles	WM	16	Boarder	35th
Robbinson, Kate	WF	35	Boarder	18th
Robinson, James	WM	14	Lodger	11th
Robinson, John	WM	15	Lodger	RIV
Rodriguez, Lizzie	WF	7	Lodger	SMP

Rogers, George	WM	18	Lodger	11th
Rogers, William	WM	14	Boarder	NWS
Romly, Thomas	WM	18	Lodger	11th
Rooney, Owen	WM	22	Servant	NWS
Rowan, Jno.	WM	15	Boarder	35th
Rudolf, William	WM	15	Lodger	18th
Rumbel, Henry	WM	17	Lodger	18th
Rush, Michael	WM	17	Lodger	18th
Russel, Lizzie	WF	9	Lodger	SMP
Ryan, Daniel	WM	18	Boarder	35th
Ryan, John	WM	18	Lodger	18th
Ryan, Michael	WM	14	Boarder	NWS
Ryan, Patrick	WM	15	Boarder	NWS
Ryan, Thomas	WM	23	Lodger	11th
Ryan, William	WM	16	Lodger	RIV
Ryder, James	WM	15	Lodger	18th
Sampson, James	WM	9	Lodger	RIV
Searls, Samuel	WM	16	Boarder	35th
Shapter, Emily	WF	4	Lodger	SMP
Sheehan, James	WM	17	Boarder	35th
Sheehan, Robert	WM	17	Lodger	RIV
Sheehan, William	WM	14	Boarder	NWS
Sheridan, James	WM	15	Boarder	NWS
Sherwood, James	WM	22	Boarder	18th
Shiels, Edward	WM	14	Boarder	NWS
Simmons, Robert	WM	18	Lodger	18th
Slater, Jeremiah	WM	6	Boarder	11th
Smallwood, Geo.	BM	12	Lodger	18th
Smith, Frank	WM	16	Lodger	RIV
Smith, Henry	WM	18	Boarder	35th
Smith, John	WM	12	Boarder	NWS
Smith, Robert	WM	18	Lodger	11th
Smith, Thomas	WM	16	Lodger	RIV
Smith, William	WM	10	Lodger	RIV
Smith, William	WM	15	Lodger	18th
Somers, David	WM	16	Boarder	NWS
Spencer, Maggie	WF	12	Lodger	SMP
Speryes, Philip	WM	16	Lodger	RIV
Spiegel, John	WM	16	Lodger	18th
Stamford, James	WM	17	Lodger	18th
Stephenson, John	BM	17	Lodger	18th

Stewart, John	WM	15	Boarder	NWS
Stout, John	WM	17	Lodger	11th
Stowbridge, Robert	WM	13	Lodger	18th
Sullivan, Charles	WM	21	Lodger	11th
Sullivan, Jeremiah	WM	16	Boarder	NWS
Sullivan, John	WM	14	Boarder	NWS
Sullivan, Thomas	WM	16	Boarder	NWS
Summers, Annie	WF	9	Lodger	SMP
Swift, Edward	WM	16	Boarder	NWS
Talbot, James	WM	15	Lodger	RIV
Taylor, William	WM	20	Lodger	11th
Thompson, John	WM	15	Boarder	NWS
Thompson, John	WM	18	Lodger	RIV
Tierney, John	WM	15	Lodger	RIV
Tierny, James	WM	16	Lodger	18th
Tighe, John	WM	17	Lodger	11th
Tingard, Henry	WM	16	Boarder	NWS
Tobfor, August	WM	16	Boarder	NWS
Toy, Charles	WM	17	Boarder	35th
Trainor, Christopher	WM	22	Lodger	11th
Turner, John J.	WM	16	Boarder	NWS
Turner, John	WM	16	Boarder	NWS
Tyner, Michael	WM	14	Boarder	35th
Virginia, Thomas	WM	16	Boarder	NWS
Walker, Fred'k.	WM	18	Lodger	18th
Walker, James	WM	18	Lodger	11th
Wallace, John	WM	17	Lodger	11th
Walsh, Charles	WM	15	Boarder	NWS
Walsh, Robert	WM	17	Lodger	RIV
Ward, Agnes J.	WF	13	Lodger	SMP
Ward, John	WM	18	Lodger	RIV
Warner, George	WM	14	Boarder	35th
Water, Horace	WM	13	Boarder	NWS
Waters, William	WM	16	Lodger	RIV
Weaver, Henry	WM	16	Boarder	NWS
Whalen, Patrick	WM	17	Boarder	NWS
White, George	WM	18	Lodger	18th
White, Patrick	WM	17	Lodger	RIV
White, William	WM	16	Boarder	35th
Whitehorn, Emily	WF	7	Lodger	SMP
Wilkens, George	WM	14	Boarder	35th

Wilkins, Thomas	WM	13	Lodger	RIV
Williams, Charles	WM	18	Lodger	RIV
Williams, Edward	WM	14	Boarder	NWS
Williams, Edward	WM	17	Boarder	NWS
Wilson, Amelia	WF	3	Lodger	SMP
Wilson, Florence	WM	14	Boarder	NWS
Wilson, George	WM	16	Servant	NWS
Wright, John	WM	12	Boarder	NWS
Wright, John	WM	14	Boarder	NWS
Yardley, Lizzie	WF	6	Lodger	SMP
Young, Fred	WM	17	Boarder	35th
Young, Robert	WM	18	Lodger	18th

1890

Guide to Column Headings

in the

1890 New York City Police Enumeration

Name Name of each person whose usual place of abode was in this institution. Surname first, then the given name and middle initial.

Sex Gender.

Age Age. Designated in years, unless otherwise noted with a "d" for "days" or an "m" for "month".

* Notes that information may have been incorrectly reported by the enumerator.

LH Lodging House. The following lodging houses were included in this census:

44th: Forty-fourth Street Lodging House
247 East 44th Street
Assembly District 20
Enumeration District 35

287: East Side Lodging House
287 Broadway
Assembly District 1
Enumeration District 14

NWS: Newsboys' Lodging House
9 Duane Street
Assembly District 14
Enumeration District 8

SMP: Girls' Lodging House
27 St. Mark's Place
Assembly District 14
Enumeration District 1

TMP: Tompkin's Square Lodging House
295 East 8th Street
Assembly District 14
Enumeration District 8

Note No other information was included in this census.

Name	G	A	LH
Addison, John	M	14	NWS
Allen, George	M	18	NWS
Allen, Oliver	M	19	NWS
Amarion, Jossie	F	15	SMP
Amarion, Lottie	F	13	SMP
Anderson, Jenny	F	22	SMP
Annigan, Harry	M	14	NWS
Anniger, William	M	17	NWS
Armstedt, Richard	M	18	NWS
Armstrong, Henry	M	18	NWS
Arrudt, John	M	15	TMP
Arstman, Arthur	M	18	NWS
Bastine, Nelia	F	28	SMP
Bauel, Louis	M	13	TMP
Beatice, Charles	M	17	NWS
Bergen, James	M	9	TMP
Bey, Maria	F	22	SMP
Blunnkett, Orville	M	17	44th
Bock, William	M	8	TMP
Brady, Annie	F	40	287
Brady, Arthur	M	7	287
Brady, Edward	M	22	287
Brady, Patrick J.	M	50	287
Brady, Philip	M	16	287
Bremen, Frank	M	18	NWS
Briggs, Henry	M	18	NWS
Brine, Nora O.	F	26	NWS
Brinkenkoff, George	M	16	NWS
Brown, Edward	M	14	TMP
Brown, Eliza	F	26	TMP
Brown, Emma	F	57	TMP
Brown, William	M	14	TMP
Brown, William	M	15	TMP
Bruhl, Carl	M	20	44th
Buching, Celia A.	F	50	SMP
Buckley, Charles	M	9	TMP
Bullien, Richard	M	20	44th
Burgess, Alfred	M	17	NWS
Burke, John	M	16	44th
Burke, Maggie	F	19	SMP
Burke, William	M	14	TMP
Burkly, Edward	M	17	TMP
Burnes, Joseph	M	17	NWS
Burns, Joseph	M	18	NWS
Burns, Mary	F	30	287
Cahn, Fred	M	17	NWS
Caldwell, Danial	M	18	NWS
Campbell, George	M	15	NWS
Carney, Thomas	M	17	NWS
Carr, James	M	20	44th
Carr, John	M	18	NWS
Carson, Samuel	M	15	TMP
Carven, Thomas	M	13	TMP
Casey, Mary	F	16	SMP
Casie, John	M	16	NWS
Clarke, Michael	M	18	NWS
Coffey, Richard	M	17	NWS
Cole, Horace	M	14	TMP
Collins, George	M	17	NWS
Collins, James	M	14	TMP
Conner, Thomas	M	19	44th
Connors, Richard	M	20	44th
Cooper, Charles	M	14	TMP
Cordon, John	M	17	NWS
Costigan, Michael	M	18	NWS
Cupps, Delia	F	43	SMP
Daphney, Edward	M	18	NWS
Darling, Florance	F	15	SMP
Darn, James	M	17	TMP
Davis, Joseph	M	16	NWS
Decker, Fred	M	15	44th

Deegan, James	M	17	44th
Demmeyer, Charles W.	M	17	NWS
Denning, George	M	21	44th
Dent, Katie	F	23	44th
Derroch, Edward	M	18	NWS
Doran, John	M	16	44th
Dounes, Mary	F	45	SMP
Dow, Patrick	M	18	NWS
Dowling, Phillips	M	13	TMP
Downs, Joshua	M	22	44th
Doyle, Peter	M	18	NWS
Duffner, Annie	F	17	SMP
Duggan, James	M	17	44th
Duncan, Edwin	M	14	TMP
Eberhart, John	M	20	NWS
Eddington, Bort	M	17	NWS
Ennis, James	M	17	NWS
Ennis, Michael	M	17	NWS
Fannigan, Michael	M	12	TMP
Fanning, James	M	17	NWS
Fay, Thomas	M	20	44th
Fehlig, Charles	M	17	NWS
Filks, Charles	M	11	TMP
Flagner, Peter	M	17	NWS
Fleishman, Lottie	F	15	SMP
Fleming, Edward	M	18	NWS
Fling, George	M	16	NWS
Flynn, Edward	M	16	44th
Fogarty, James	M	20	44th
Foley, Frank	M	19	44th
Frazier, John	M	18	NWS
Gale, Frederick	M	22	44th
Galvin, John	M	18	NWS
Gavlin, James	M	17	44th
Gerger, James	M	10	TMP
Gleason, John	M	22	44th
Goodwin, William	M	16	NWS
Gregonira, Amelia	F	7	SMP
Gregory, John	M	17	NWS
Gremmel, August	M	9	TMP
Griffen, Hanry	M	15	44th
Grynan, Maggie	F	14	SMP
Hacht, David	M	14	TMP
Hadelson, Ike	M	17	NWS
Haggerty, James	M	17	44th
Hamill, Hugh	M	32	NWS
Hana, Denis	M	16	NWS
Handlon, John	M	18	NWS
Hankey, Thomas	M	19	44th
Hannegan, James	M	15	NWS
Hanrahan, James	M	17	NWS
Hansee, Jacob	M	8	TMP
Harris, William	M	13	TMP
Harrison, Anna	F	17	SMP
Hartnett, Thomas	M	17	TMP
Hayes, James	M	14	NWS
Hayes, Loucia	F	17	SMP
Hayes, Mary	F	18	44th
Hayes, Mary	F	60	44th
Hayes, Thomas	M	18	NWS
Hearly, John	M	18	NWS
Hearn, James	M	17	NWS
Heffernan, Henry	M	14	44th
Heig, Andrew F.	M	7m	NWS
Heig, Augusta	F	29	NWS
Heig, Oscar J.	M	2	NWS
Heig, Rudolph J.	M	3	NWS
Heig, Rudolph	M	27	NWS
Hendrix, Jacob	M	18	NWS
Higgins, Thomas	M	18	NWS
Hoffmann, Benjamin	M	13	TMP
Hogan, James	M	15	TMP

Name	Sex	Age	
Hoitt, David	M	17	NWS
Horne, William E.	M	17	NWS
Howitz, Jacob	M	17	NWS
Hurley, Elizabeth S.	F	63	SMP
Hynes, Thomas	M	18	NWS
Johnson, Edward	M	18	44th
Jordan, James	M	16	44th
Keating, John	M	17	NWS
Kegan, William	M	15	NWS
Kelleo, Charles	M	16	TMP
Kelly, Frank	M	17	44th
Kelly, John	M	17	NWS
Kelly, John	M	18	NWS
Kelly, John	M	30	44th
Kelly, Joseph	M	14	NWS
Kelly, William	M	16	44th
Kelly, William	M	17	44th
Kennedy, Danial	M	18	NWS
Kennedy, Gordon	M	20	44th
Kennedy, John	M	14	NWS
Keohen, Patrick	M	16	NWS
Kiernan, John	M	16	NWS
Kies, Edward	M	7	TMP
Knight, Fred	M	13	NWS
Knoblaugh, Harry	M	8	TMP
Koch, Henry	M	16	NWS
Kogers, Charles	M	17	NWS
Larmonie, Josephine	F	18	SMP
Larmonie, Mary	F	16	SMP
Leary, Katie	F	17	NWS
Lee, Gim	M	70	SMP
Lee, Mary	F	12	SMP
Lenahan, John	M	18	NWS
Liebenlist, Lewis	M	16	NWS
Loeb, Lizza	F	19	SMP
Long, William	M	13	TMP
Mace, George	M	18	NWS
Madden, Thomas	M	13	TMP
Madden, Thomas	M	15	NWS
Mahoney, James	M	22	44th
Malaye, John	M	14	NWS
Malloney, John	M	18	NWS
Mann, John	M	19	44th
Martin, James	M	18	44th
Matthew, Alice	F	3	44th
Matthew, Editz	F	9	44th
Matthew, Emma	F	36	44th
Matthew, William	M	46	44th
Matzler, John	M	33	TMP
McArthur, Ann	F	54	44th
McCall, John	M	13	TMP
McCormack, John	M	16	44th
McCoy, John	M	16	TMP
McDonald, Dennis	M	20	44th
McDonald, Dennis	M	21	44th
McDonald, John	M	19	44th
McDonald, Samuel	M	22	44th
McGahn, Hugh	M	26	44th
McGee, Thomas	M	17	NWS
McGill, Jenny	F	21	SMP
McGuiness, James	M	17	NWS
McGuinness, John	M	18	NWS
McIntyre, Annie	F	31	SMP
McKenna, James	M	18	44th
McKenna, John	M	17	TMP
McLaughlin, Thomas	M	14	TMP
McNay, Sarah	F	17	SMP
Meehan, Eliza	F	36	TMP
Mehrtens, William	M	10	TMP
Meyer, John	M	15	TMP

Meyer, Robert	M	16	44th
Meyer, Thomas	M	22	44th
Michal, Louise	F	14	SMP
Miller, George	M	17	NWS
Miller, Henry	M	17	NWS
Monk, James	M	19	44th
Montgomery, Rose	F	15	SMP
Moore, William	M	15	TMP
Moran, William	M	16	44th
Morell, Louis	M	17	44th
Morgan, Thomas	M	17	44th
Morrill, Elizabeth	F	45	SMP
Morris, James	M	18	NWS
Morrisey, James	M	16	44th
Morrisy, James	M	18	NWS
Mortan, William	M	17	NWS
Mortimer, Fred	M	18	NWS
Muldoon, Peter	M	15	NWS
Mullen, Peter	M	22	44th
Mulligan, Charles	M	15	44th
Mulling, Leon	M	12	TMP
Mulvey, John	M	17	NWS
Murphy, Danial	M	17	NWS
Murphy, James	M	13	TMP
Murphy, James	M	14	TMP
Murphy, James	M	15	NWS
Murray, Bernard	M	13	TMP
Murray, Bernard	M	15	TMP
Murray, Louis	M	19	44th
Murray, Thomas	M	16	TMP
Murtagh, Jossie	F	15	SMP
Nay, Thomas	M	18	NWS
Noe, George	M	17	NWS
Nutall, Amy	F	17	SMP
O'Brine, John	M	17	NWS
O'Brine, John	M	18	NWS
O'Connell, Fred	M	18	NWS
O'Conor, John	M	15	NWS
O'Conor, John	M	17	NWS
O'Conor, Michael	M	15	NWS
O'Conor, William	M	15	NWS
Odessa, Mary	F	8	SMP
O'Keefe, Dennis	M	18	44th
O'Keefe, James	M	17	44th
O'Keefe, Robert	M	17	44th
O'Neil, James	M	18	NWS
O'Neil, John	M	18	NWS
O'Rourke, Thomas	M	-	44th
Orr, William	M	18	44th
Ortel, Wm.	M	14	TMP
O'Shaughnessy, Joseph	M	17	TMP
O'Toole, Edward	M	19	44th
O'Toole, Lawrence	M	20	44th
Palmer, John	M	17	NWS
Plunkett, Charles	M	10	TMP
Power, Katie	F	22	NWS
Quinn, Thomas	M	17	NWS
Ray, F. B.	M	18	NWS
Reardon, Fred	M	14	TMP
Reddy, Thomas	M	17	NWS
Regan, James	M	17	44th
Regan, Thomas	M	17	NWS
Reilly, James	M	17	NWS
Reilly, John	M	11	TMP
Reilly, John	M	14	TMP
Reinan, Elise	F	13	SMP
Reynolds, Fredrick	M	15	TMP
Reynolds, Fredrick	M	17	TMP
Reynolds, George	M	25	NWS
Reynolds, Walter	M	13	TMP

Rielly, George	M	12	TMP
Riley, John	M	15	44th
Robbin, Lizza	F	16	SMP
Robinson, Peter	M	17	NWS
Roche, John	M	18	NWS
Rogers, Benjamin	M	12	TMP
Rondell, Lidia	F	15	SMP
Rooney, James	M	18	NWS
Royal, Mary	F	19	NWS
Ryan, Danial	M	17	NWS
Ryan, John	M	17	TMP
Ryan, William	M	18	NWS
Salter, James	M	19	44th
Samuel, John	M	18	NWS
Sauwer, Englehart	M	33	TMP
Sauwer, Katy	F	2	TMP
Sauwer, Sophy	F	25	TMP
Scammel, Julia	F	34	SMP
Schinberger, Charles	M	17	NWS
Schokes, Henry	M	15	44th
Schwartz, Margarett	F	25	TMP
Scott, Winifred	M	32	TMP
Seignor, Elsia	F	13	SMP
Sevirburg, Harris	M	16	NWS
Shaffer, Anna	F	45	SMP
Shawger, Frances	F	16	SMP
Shay, Tim	M	16	NWS
Sherry, William	M	16	44th
Shield, Joseph	M	18	NWS
Siegel, Charles	M	16	TMP
Sigel, Antonia	F	10	SMP
Silvester, Charles	M	18	NWS
Sloene, Anne	F	40	NWS
Smith, Charles	M	14	TMP
Smith, Charles	M	15	TMP
Smith, Charles	M	18	NWS
Smith, Harry	M	19	44th
Smith, Harry	M	20	44th
Smith, Henry	M	11	TMP
Smith, James	M	18	NWS
Smith, John	M	14	NWS
Smith, John	M	16	NWS
Stirder, Martha	F	16	SMP
Stoffel, Adam E.	M	33	NWS
Stone, Charles	M	17	NWS
Sullivan, Arthur	M	17	NWS
Sullivan, John	M	12	TMP
Sullivan, John	M	13	TMP
Sullivan, Joseph	M	21	44th
Sweeney, John	M	17	NWS
Sweeney, John	M	18	NWS
Taylor, Gus	M	13	TMP
Thompson, Matty	M	13	NWS
Tishouser, Minnie	F	30	TMP
Tower, John	M	16	44th
Townsend, Thomas	M	16	44th
Toy, Walter	M	18	44th
Trettner, Alander	M	17	NWS
Troutman, John	M	18	NWS
Vesto, Henry	M	10	TMP
Walch, John	M	17	NWS
Walch, Michael	M	18	NWS
Walsh, Edward	M	7	TMP
Washburn, Charles	M	24	NWS
Webery, Harry	M	15	NWS
Weiss, Alfred	M	14	TMP
Welsh, James	M	12	TMP
White, Charles	M	16	NWS
White, George	M	16	NWS
Whiting, Edward	M	17	NWS

Wickfall, Edward	M	18	NWS
Wilde, James	M	18	NWS
Williams, Fred	M	17	NWS
Williams, George	M	17	NWS
Wilson, Amelia	F	36	SMP
Winters, Annie	F	17	44th
Winters, Fanny	F	19	44th
Yardley, Lizza	F	44	SMP
Ylemann, Thomas	M	15	TMP
Young, Charles	M	13	TMP
Young, James	M	18	44th

1900

Guide to Column Headings

in the

1900 Federal Enumeration

Name	Name of each person whose usual place of abode was in the institution on June 1, 1900. The census includes the name of every person living on June 1, 1900. Children born since June 1, 1900 were omitted. The surname is listed first, then the given name and middle initial.
R-G	Race and gender. "White" is designated by "W", "Black" by "B", and "Mulatto" by "Mu". "Males" are designated by "M" and "Females" by "F".
*	Notes that the enumerator may have reported the information incorrectly.
A	Age at last birthday. Designated in years, unless otherwise noted with an "m" for "months".
M	Month of birth.
Y	Year of birth.
Relation	Relationship of each person to the institution.

LH Lodging House. The following lodging houses were included in this census:

44th: Forty-fourth Street Lodging House
247 East 44th Street
Enumeration District 581

BMF: Brace Memorial Farm
Valhalla, Mount Pleasant,
Westchester County
Enumeration District 76

EHG: Elizabeth Home for Girls
307 East 12th Street
Enumeration District 323

FGG: Fogg Lodging House
552 West 53rd Street
Enumeration District 404

NWS: Newsboys' Lodging House
9 Duane Street
Enumeration District 24

TMP: Tompkin's Square Lodging House
295 East 8th Street
Enumeration District 339

WSB: West Side Boys' Lodging House
201 West 32nd Street
Enumeration District 254

Note Refer to the orginal census for the birthplace of each occupant and his or her parents.

Name	R-G	M	Year	A	Relation	LH
Abbott, Fred	WM	unk.	1891	9	Inmate	BMF
Ahearn, John	WM	Sept.	1883	16	Lodger	NWS
Albee, Abbie, R.	WF	Nov.	1833	66	Seamstress	BMF
Alfonsa, Frank	WM	July	1883	16	Janitor	44th
Alton, Agnes	WF	unk.	unk.	15	Inmate	EHG
Ambridge, Lulu	WF	unk.	unk.	19	Inmate	EHG
Andersen, Rob't.	BM	Nov.	1884	15	Lodger	NWS
Angelina, Charles	WM	Apr.	1885	15	Lodger	TMP
Ashton, Grace	WF	unk.	unk.	15	Inmate	EHG
Aspin, John	WM	June	1843	56	Lodger	NWS
Auckland, Willie	WM	unk.	1890	10	Inmate	BMF
Austin, John	WM	Jan.	1882	18	Lodger	44th
Backer, John	WM	Mar.	1883	17	Lodger	44th
Bailey, Louis R.	WM	July	1878	22	Day Watchman	WSB
Baker, Edwin	WM	July	1882	17	Lodger	44th
Bantz, Joseph	WM	Nov.	1883	16	Lodger	NWS
Barnes, Rowan	BM	Mar.	1882	18	Lodger	44th
Beck, Peter	WM	Aug.	1881	18	Inmate	WSB
Becker, Oscar	WM	Nov.	1882	18*	Lodger	44th
Becok, Daniel	WM	Mar.	1881	18	Lodger	NWS
Beeir, Charles	WM	May	1883	17	Lodger	TMP
Benedict, Robert	WM	Jan.	1883	17	Inmate	WSB
Benner, Robert A.	WM	Aug.	1884	15	Lodger	TMP
Benton, Cornelia	WF	unk.	unk.	19	Inmate	EHG
Bernard, James	WM	Feb.	1881	19	Lodger	NWS
Bird, Michael	WM	Sept.	1883	16	Lodger	TMP
Blair, Richard	WM	June	1884	15	Lodger	TMP
Blanc, Joseph	WM	Mar.	1882	18	Lodger	44th
Blenis, Charles R.	WM	Aug.	1870	29	Help	TMP
Bloomfield, Chas.	WM	Jan.	1886	16	Lodger	NWS
Bomgard, Willis	WM	Apr.	1883	17	Inmate	WSB
Bouer, Chester	WM	unk.	1894	6	Inmate	BMF
Boyle, Thomas	WM	Dec.	1880	19	Inmate	WSB
Boyle, Thomas	WM	Nov.	1884	15	Inmate	WSB
Boysen, Frank	WM	unk.	1882	18	Inmate	WSB
Brennan, Thomas	WM	July	1882	18	Inmate	WSB
Brennan, Thos.	WM	July	1885	14	Lodger	44th
Broderick, John	WM	Apr.	1883	17	Inmate	WSB
Brown, Charles H.	WM	Nov.	1856	43	Help	TMP

Brown, Edward	WM	Feb.	1882	18	Inmate	WSB
Brown, Frank	WM	unk.	1886	14	Inmate	BMF
Brown, James F.	WM	Feb.	1883	17	Inmate	WSB
Brown, Margaret	WF	Feb.	1833	67	Help	TMP
Brown, Robert	WM	Oct.	1887	13	Inmate	BMF
Brown, William	WM	June	1887	12	Lodger	TMP
Brundage, Willis	WM	unk.	1894	6	Inmate	BMF
Bryant, Carl	WM	unk.	1894	6	Inmate	BMF
Burds, Joseph	WM	Mar.	1882	18	Lodger	44th
Burns, Fannie	WF	unk.	unk.	20	Inmate	EHG
Bushnell, John	WM	June	1883	16	Lodger	TMP
Call, Cora M.	WF	Mar.	1894	6	Daughter	BMF
Call, David E.	WM	Aug.	1868	31	Caretaker	BMF
Call, Joel F.	WM	Feb.	1896	4	Son	BMF
Call, Myrtle M.	WF	Sept.	1875	24	Laundress	BMF
Campbell, Wm.	BM	July	1882	17	Lodger	NWS
Carey, Frank	WM	April	1883	17	Lodger	TMP
Carey, James	WM	April	1883	17	Lodger	TMP
Carlitto, Geonree	WM	unk.	1890	10	Inmate	BMF
Carney, Irvington	WM	unk.	1894	6	Inmate	BMF
Carpenter, Flora	WF	Dec.	1872	28	Cook	WSB
Carroll, John	WM	Aug.	1882	17	Lodger	44th
Carter, William	WM	Mar.	1883	17	Lodger	44th
Cassidy, Timothy J.	WM	Sept.	1882	17	Lodger	NWS
Chase, Minnie	WF	unk.	unk.	16	Inmate	EHG
Christian, Christianna	WF	unk.	unk.	18	Inmate	EHG
Clancy, James J.	WM	Aug.	1870	29	Caretaker	BMF
Clancy, Mary R.	WF	Mar.	1861	39	Cook	BMF
Clare, George	WM	May	1881	19	Lodger	44th
Clark, Edward	WM	Aug.	1882	17	Lodger	TMP
Clark, James	WM	July	1883	17	Inmate	WSB
Clark, Simon	WM	June	1886	13	Inmate	BMF
Clien, Edward	WM	June	1883	16	Inmate	BMF
Coffy, James	WM	June	1884	15	Lodger	44th
Cohen, Samuel	WM	Jan.	1884	16	Lodger	NWS
Coile, William	WM	Sept.	1882	17	Lodger	TMP
Coleman, William	WM	May	1881	19	Lodger	NWS
Collins, August J.	WM	June	1882	18	Inmate	WSB
Colrow, George	WM	May	1882	18	Inmate	WSB
Connely, Joseph	WM	June.	1882	17	Lodger	TMP

Connors, Barton	WM	Sept.	1891	18	Lodger	TMP
Connors, Richard	WM	Apr.	1871	29	Watchman	44th
Conny, Harry	WM	Feb.	1882	18	Lodger	NWS
Conogan, Charles	WM	unk.	1890	10	Inmate	BMF
Cook, Roy	WM	unk.	1894	6	Inmate	BMF
Cook, Wesley	WM	unk.	1893	7	Inmate	BMF
Corley, Samuel	WM	Feb.	1894	6	Lodger	44th
Corrigan, John	WM	Jun.	1881	18	Lodger	44th
Cosley, Samuel	WM	unk.	1896	4	Inmate	BMF
Coswell, Thomas	WM	Aug.	1881	18	Lodger	NWS
Crane, Joseph	WM	unk.	1893	7	Inmate	BMF
Cullen, James J.	WM	Nov.	1883	16	Lodger	TMP
Cummins, Benj.	WM	Mar.	1882	18	Lodger	NWS
Curlew, Lillian	WF	unk.	unk.	15	Inmate	EHG
Curley, Thomas	WM	unk.	1882	18	Inmate	WSB
Curr, Frank	WM	Mar.	1883	17	Lodger	44th
Curtis, Felix	WM	unk.	1893	7	Inmate	BMF
Curtis, John	WM	unk.	1889	11	Inmate	BMF
Dadie, Joseph	WM	June	1882	17	Lodger	NWS
Dailey, Elmer	WM	unk.	1891	9	Inmate	BMF
Deacon, Margaret	WF	unk.	unk.	17	Inmate	EHG
Deary, Thomas D.	WM	May	1882	18	Lodger	NWS
Devlin, John	WM	Sept.	1884	15	Lodger	44th
Devoe, James	WM	unk.	1891	9	Inmate	BMF
Dodd, Wm.	WM	Apr.	1882	18	Lodger	NWS
Downs, Thos.	WM	Mar.	1884	16	Lodger	NWS
Doyle, Bernard	WM	unk.	1884	16	Inmate	BMF
Duffey, John	WM	unk.	1883	17	Inmate	WSB
Duffy, John	WM	Aug.	1883	16	Lodger	44th
Dundon, James	WM	Mar.	1884	16	Inmate	WSB
Eckhoff, Walter	WM	unk.	1894	6	Inmate	BMF
Edgerson, Walter C.	WM	Mar.	1879	21	Engineer	BMF
Elston, Elijah, B.	WM	Oct.	1872	28	Engineer	WSB
Enheven, George	WM	unk.	1890	10	Inmate	BMF
Ewald, Kate	WF	unk.	unk.	18	Inmate	EHG
Farrell, Charles	WM	Apr.	1883	17	Lodger	44th
Farrell, Charles	WM	Dec.	1880	19	Lodger	44th
Farrell, Daniel	WM	Aug.	1883	16	Lodger	44th
Fassberg, Louis	WM	Sept.	1885	14	Lodger	NWS
Feister, Mary	WF	unk.	unk.	14	Inmate	EHG
Fennell, Michael	WM	June	1882	17	Lodger	TMP

Fergurson, Philip	WM	May	1885	15	Inmate	WSB
Feron, John	WM	Apr.	1882	18	Lodger	44th
Fisher, Charles P.	WM	May	1870	30	Help	TMP
Fitzgerald, George	WM	Dec.	1888	11	Inmate	WSB
Fitzpatrick, Hugh	WM	July	1883	17	Lodger	NWS
Flanigan, John	WM	June	1883	17	Inmate	WSB
Flannighan, John	WM	unk.	1891	9	Inmate	BMF
Fleming, John	WM	Dec.	1883	16	Inmate	WSB
Forbes, Frederick	WM	July	1882	17	Lodger	TMP
Freedmann, Chas.	WM	Dec.	1884	15	Lodger	NWS
Freigel, Ira	WM	Nov.	1882	17	Lodger	44th
Fuller, Tony	BM	May	1884	16	Lodger	TMP
Gaughan, Mary	WF	Jan.	1879	21	Waitress	WSB
Germay, Francis	WM	July	1882	17	Lodger	NWS
Gerrity, John	WM	Jan.	1881	19	Lodger	44th
Gilbey, Joseph	WM	June	1882	17	Lodger	44th
Gilligan, Joseph	WM	Oct.	1882	17	Lodger	TMP
Gilmartin, John	WM	May	1884	16	Inmate	WSB
Gleason, Harry	WM	unk.	1893	7	Inmate	BMF
Glennon, Thomas	WM	unk.	1890	10	Inmate	WSB
Goff, Eva	WF	Jan.	1840	40	Matron	BMF
Goff, Floyd	WM	Mar.	1860	40	Superintendant	BMF
Goghan, Patrick	WM	Oct.	1882	17	Lodger	NWS
Goldberg, Jos.	WM	July	1884	15	Lodger	NWS
Golden, Jack	WM	unk.	1883	17	Inmate	WSB
Goldstein, Himan	WM	May	1884	15*	Lodger	NWS
Goodwin, Mary	WF	May	1865	35	Laundress	WSB
Gourley, Carlitto	WM	unk.	1890	10	Inmate	BMF
Gray, Arthur	WM	unk.	1892	8	Inmate	BMF
Green, Henry	WM	Jan.	1881	19	Inmate	WSB
Green, John	WM	Nov.	1883	16	Lodger	NWS
Greenberg, Harry	WM	Jan.	1884	16	Inmate	WSB
Greenberg, Louis	WM	May	1884	16	Inmate	WSB
Gronginskey, Abe	WM	Dec.	1881	18	Lodger	NWS
Grosvenor, William	WM	March	1865	35	Head	TMP
Grunan, Patrick	WM	July	1884	15	Inmate	WSB
Hadden, Lillian	WF	unk	unk.	16	Inmate	EHG
Haft, David	WM	Mar.	1884	16	Inmate	BMF
Hagen, Owen	WM	Sept.	1882	17	Lodger	44th
Haggerty, Frank	WM	Nov.	1882	17	Lodger	TMP
Hahn, Charles	WM	unk.	1889	11	Inmate	BMF

Halfpenny, C.J.	WM	Feb.	1882	18	Lodger	NWS
Hampel, Katie	WF	unk.	unk.	15	Inmate	EHG
Hank, Albert	WM	Oct.	1883	16	Lodger	TMP
Harbor, Joseph	WM	July	1884	15	Lodger	TMP
Harrington, John	WM	May	1883	17	Inmate	WSB
Harris, Joseph	WM	Sept.	1883	16	Lodger	TMP
Haspel, Jacob	WM	Nov.	1883	17	Lodger	TMP
Hattin, John	WM	June	1881	19	Inmate	WSB
Hayes, Clifford	WM	Dec.	1882	17	Lodger	NWS
Hays, David	WM	Feb.	1884	16	Inmate	WSB
Healey, John Frank	WM	Oct.	1884	15	Inmate	WSB
Heig, Augusta M.	WF	Jun.	1861	38	Lodger	NWS
Heig, Rudolph	WM	Jan.	1864	36	Lodger	NWS
Henderson, Peter	WM	Nov.	1880	19	Lodger	NWS
Hendron, Joseph	WM	July	1886	13	Inmate	BMF
Hendron, Mark	WM	unk.	1888	12	Inmate	BMF
Hennessy, William	WM	Apr.	1884	16	Inmate	WSB
Herbertson, Edwin	WM	Sept.	1884	15	Inmate	BMF
Herbst, Harry	WM	Apr.	1884	16	Inmate	WSB
Hester, James	WM	Sept.	1883	16	Lodger	44th
Hickather, Charles	WM	Oct.	1881	18	Inmate	WSB
Higgins, John	WM	May	1884	16	Lodger	NWS
Hirshfield, Jacob	WM	June	1883	16	Lodger	NWS
Hoder, Edward	WM	Nov.	1881	18	Lodger	44th
Hodgins, Thos.	WM	June	1882	17	Lodger	NWS
Hoffman, Frank	WM	July	1883	16	Lodger	TMP
Hoffmann, A.	WM	Nov.	1881	18	Lodger	NWS
Holdmann, Fred.	WM	July	1886	13	Inmate	BMF
Hollingsworth, Anne	WF	unk.	unk.	17	Inmate	EHG
Horan, Wm.	WM	Oct.	1881	18	Lodger	NWS
Howe, William	BM	July	1883	16	Lodger	NWS
Huff, Barbara	WF	unk.	unk.	20	Inmate	EHG
Hughson, Wm. B.	WM	Apr.	1866	34	Asst. Super.	WSB
Hulse, Lottie	WF	unk.	unk.	15	Inmate	EHG
Humphrey, Calvin	WM	unk.	1894	6	Inmate	BMF
Humphrey, William	WM	unk.	1891	9	Inmate	BMF
Hunter, Richard	WM	Jan.	1884	16	Inmate	BMF
Hurley, Elizabeth	WF	Jan.	1827	73	Matron	EHG
Jackson, Chas.	BM	May	1882	18	Lodger	NWS
Jackson, Joseph	BM	Feb.	1883	17	Inmate	WSB

Jackson, Louis	WM	July	1881	18	Lodger	TMP
Jacob, Chas.	WM	May	1883	17	Lodger	NWS
Janors, Abraham	WM	June	1884	15	Lodger	TMP
Jayne, David E.	WM	July	1880	20	Watchman	WSB
Jerry, Eliz.	WF	Apr.	1854	46	Boarder	FGG
Johanson, Oli	WM	Oct.	1881	18	Lodger	44th
Johnson, Annie	WF	unk.	unk.	21	Inmate	EHG
Johnson, John	WM	June	1883	16	Lodger	NWS
Johnson, May	WF	unk.	unk.	15	Inmate	EHG
Johnson, Minnie	WF	unk.	unk.	14	Inmate	EHG
Jones, James	WM	Nov.	1883	17	Inmate	WSB
Jones, William	WM	Aug.	1883	16	Lodger	44th
Jorden, John	BM	Oct.	1883	16	Inmate	WSB
Joulseky, James	WM	Nov.	1883	16	Inmate	WSB
Katz, Samuel	WM	Sept.	1885	14	Lodger	NWS
Kaughran, Jennie	WF	unk.	unk.	15	Inmate	EHG
Keating, John	WM	Sept.	1882	17	Inmate	WSB
Kelley, John	WM	Feb.	1884	16	Lodger	44th
Kelly, Frank	WM	Nov.	1883	16	Inmate	WSB
Kennedy, Jas.	WM	June	1882	17	Lodger	NWS
Keough, John	WM	July	1884	15	Lodger	NWS
Kern, John	WM	Apr.	1887	13	Inmate	BMF
Kerr, Robert E.	BM	Jan.	1884	16	Lodger	44th
Kersham, John	WM	Jan.	1883	17	Lodger	44th
Ketchum, Rose	WF	unk.	unk.	14	Inmate	EHG
Kibbin, Hannah	WF	Feb.	1844	56	Matron	BMF
Kiernan, James	WM	May	1882	18	Lodger	44th
Kilburg, Alfred H.	WM	Dec.	1872	28	Farm Laborer	BMF
Kilburg, Cora A.	WF	Aug.	1874	25	Servant	BMF
Kinhelm, August	WM	unk.	1890	10	Inmate	BMF
Kinner, Rachel	WF	unk.	unk.	18	Inmate	EHG
Kirschbaum, Jacob	WM	Sept.	1883	16	Lodger	TMP
Klein, Geo.	WM	Mar.	1883	17	Lodger	NWS
Knowles, Willi	WM	unk.	1892	8	Inmate	BMF
Knox, Jennie	WF	unk.	unk.	15	Inmate	EHG
Kopolovitch, Wm.	WM	April	1883	17	Lodger	NWS
Kosseff, Benjamin	WM	July	1883	16	Lodger	NWS
Krans, Daniel	WM	Jul	1883	16	Lodger	44th
Lane, Henry	WM	unk.	1888	12	Inmate	BMF
Langton, Daniel	WM	Oct.	1881	18	Lodger	44th

Lasson, Abraham	WM	Apr.	1893	7	Inmate	WSB
Laughlin, Thomas	WM	Apr.	1868	32	Head	NWS
Launtenberger, Fred	WM	Aug.	1888	11	Inmate	WSB
Leay, Thomas	WM	Mar.	1883	17	Lodger	44th
Lee, Joseph H.	WM	July	1882	17	Lodger	NWS
Leeri, William	WM	Dec.	1881	19	Inmate	WSB
Leonhardt, Rob't.	WM	Jan.	1885	15	Inmate	BMF
Lesner, Barbara	WF	unk.	unk.	17	Inmate	EHG
Levin, Otto	WM	Sept.	1883	16	Inmate	WSB
Lister, Abraham	WM	June	1885	14	Lodger	TMP
Little, Leonard	WM	Nov.	1882	17	Lodger	44th
Long, James	WM	Mar.	1882	18	Lodger	NWS
Louvain, William	WM	Nov.	1883	16	Lodger	44th
Lowerie, Elinda	WF	unk.	unk.	20	Inmate	EHG
Lutz, Julia	WF	Aug.	1871	28	Servant	NWS
Lynch, Martin	WM	Mar.	1882	18	Lodger	NWS
Lyons, Clarence	WM	unk.	1893	7	Inmate	BMF
Maas, Henry	WM	May	1884	16	Lodger	44th
Magnus, James	WM	June	1884	15	Inmate	WSB
Mahoney, James	WM	Jul.	1882	17	Lodger	44th
Malone, Jos.	WM	Feb.	1884	13	Lodger	NWS
Mandeis, Nicholas	WM	unk.	1884	15	Inmate	WSB
Manshow, Ben. J.	WM	Feb.	1881	19	Lodger	44th
Marhews, Thomas	WM	Nov.	1884	15	Lodger	44th
Marshall, Linda	WF	Aug.	1861	38	Help	TMP
Martin, Charles	WM	May	1883	17	Lodger	TMP
May, John	WM	June	1883	17	Inmate	WSB
McBee, Maggie A.	WF	Nov.	1860	39	Help	TMP
McCabe, Thomas	WM	July	1882	17	Lodger	TMP
McCall, John	WM	Apr.	1883	17	Inmate	WSB
McCall, Wm.	WM	Oct.	1882	17	Lodger	NWS
McCarthy, Kate	WF	Oct.	1871	28	Chambermaid	WSB
McCindy, William	WM	Jan.	1883	17	Lodger	NWS
McCormack, John	WM	May	1882	18	Inmate	WSB
McDonald, Arthur	WM	Mar.	1885	15	Lodger	TMP
McDonald, Arthur	WM	Nov.	1883	16	Lodger	44th
McGinnis, Dav.	WM	Jan.	1884	16	Lodger	NWS
McGuire, Frank	WM	Apr.	1886	14	Lodger	TMP
McInez, William	WM	unk.	1889	11	Inmate	BMF
McInroy, John	WM	unk.	1889	11	Inmate	BMF

McInroy, Wm.	WM	Dec.	1888	11	Lodger	NWS
McIntyre, Annie	WF	unk.	unk.	36	Inmate	EHG
McKakan, James	WM	Sept.	1881	18	Lodger	NWS
McLoughlin, Thomas	WM	unk.	1882	18	Inmate	BMF
McNamara, Jennie	WF	unk.	unk.	13	Inmate	EHG
McTermott, Patrick	WM	Mar.	1896	14	Inmate	BMF
Meehan, Elizabeth M.	WF	July	1856	43	Help	TMP
Miller, Frederick	WM	Apr.	1884	16	Lodger	TMP
Milman, Earnest	WM	unk.	1892	8	Inmate	BMF
Minder, Harry	WM	June	1882	17	Lodger	NWS
Mitnick, Walter	WM	Mar.	1885	15	Lodger	NWS
Montegue, John	WM	May	1882	18	Lodger	44th
Moore, Charles	WM	Mar.	1882	18	Lodger	TMP
Moore, Robert	WM	Jan.	1883	17	Lodger	TMP
Moore, Robert	WM	Mar.	1884	16	Lodger	44th
Morris, James	WM	Dec.	1884	15	Lodger	TMP
Morrison, Fred'k.	WM	Dec.	1883	16	Lodger	44th
Morse, Lillian	WF	unk.	unk.	15	Inmate	EHG
Muller, Louis	WM	Mar.	1887	13	Lodger	TMP
Mullin, Joseph	WM	Apr.	1883	17	Inmate	WSB
Munsey, Addie	WF	unk.	unk.	14	Inmate	EHG
Murphy, Thomas	WM	Sept.	1881	18	Lodger	NWS
Murray, James	WM	Apr.	1884	16	Inmate	WSB
Murray, John	WM	May	1881	19	Lodger	44th
Murtagh, Katie	WF	unk.	unk.	16	Inmate	EHG
Neddleton, Harry	WM	June	1884	15	Lodger	NWS
Neligin, Annie	WF	unk.	unk.	18	Inmate	EHG
Nelson, Barney	WM	unk.	1892	8	Inmate	BMF
Nelson, Charles	WM	unk.	1889	11	Inmate	BMF
Nolan, Harry	WM	June	1886	13	Lodger	NWS
Nubert, Lawrence	WM	Sept.	1883	16	Lodger	44th
Oats, John	WM	unk.	1885	15	Inmate	BMF
O'Brien, Charles	WM	Jan.	1884	16	Lodger	TMP
OConnor, Chas.	WM	Oct.	1883	16	Inmate	WSB
Offer, Morris	WM	Feb.	1884	16	Lodger	TMP
Oliver, LeRoy	BM	Apr.	1882	18	Lodger	NWS
O'Nell, Joseph J.	WM	Oct.	1882	17	Lodger	NWS
Otts, Bertha	WF	unk.	unk.	21	Inmate	EHG

Paul, Allen	WM	Aug.	1882	18	Inmate	WSB
Perrin, Paul	WM	Aug.	1885	14	Lodger	44th
Petrie, George	WM	unk.	1892	8	Inmate	BMF
Porter, Samuel	WM	Mar.	1881	19	Lodger	44th
Preston, Harold	WM	Jan.	1883	17	Lodger	44th
Quackenbush, Margaret	WF	unk.	unk.	14	Inmate	EHG
Radin, Louis	WM	July	1887	12	Lodger	NWS
Ranahan, James	WM	Jan.	1882	18	Lodger	TMP
Rannan, James	WM	June	1882	17	Lodger	TMP
Rapelyea, Roosa	WM	May	1886	14	Inmate	BMF
Ratkin, Jacob	WM	Mar.	1883	17	Lodger	NWS
Redden, Frank	WM	July	1885	14	Lodger	TMP
Redden, John	WM	May	1894*	16	Lodger	TMP
Reddy, Bridget	WF	June	1849	50	Servant	NWS
Rediken, James	WM	Dec.	1883	17*	Inmate	BMF
Reilley, John	WM	July	1885	14	Lodger	NWS
Reilly, Robert	WM	Nov.	1885	14	Lodger	TMP
Reilly, Thomas	WM	Aug.	1883	16	Lodger	TMP
Reilly, Thomas	WM	Mar.	1885	15	Lodger	44th
Reynolds, Frank	WM	Sept.	1882	17	Lodger	44th
Rielly, Thomas	WM	Mar.	1885	15	Inmate	WSB
Roanan, Timothy	WM	illeg.	1880	19	Teamster	BMF
Robertson, An.	WF	Aug.	1854	45	Janitor	FGG
Robertson, Anne	WF	Mar.	1883	17	Dressmaker	FGG
Robertson, Jean	WF	July	1881	19	College	FGG
Rooney, Alice	WF	Apr.	1871	29	Servant	NWS
Roosa, Perry D.	WM	July	1880	19	Janitor	44th
Rosen, Samuel	WM	Feb.	1884	16	Lodger	TMP
Rosenberg, Henry	WM	Mar.	1882	18	Lodger	NWS
Rosenberg, Max	WM	April	1884	16	Lodger	TMP
Rosenheimer, Abraham	WM	May	1886	14	Lodger	TMP
Ross, Chas.	WM	Jun.	1884	15	Lodger	NWS
Ruben, Eli	WM	Feb.	1884	16	Lodger	TMP
Russel, Bessie	WF	unk.	unk.	15	Inmate	EHG
Sadley, John	WM	Mar.	1883	17	Inmate	BMF
Salter, Fred	WM	Dec.	1882	17	Inmate	WSB
Sawyer, Everett J.	WM	Aug.	1879	20	Farm Laborer	BMF
Schaffer, Jacob	WM	unk.	1884	16	Inmate	BMF
Schafter, Jacob	WM	June	1882	17	Lodger	NWS

Schliephake, Freda	WF	Feb.	1885	15	Inmate	BMF
Schmidt, Joseph	WM	Nov.	1882	17	Inmate	WSB
Scholars, Michael	WM	Aug.	1888	11	Lodger	NWS
Schuabrick, Nathan	WM	Aug.	1883	16	Lodger	TMP
Scully, Willie	WM	Feb.	1890	10	Inmate	WSB
Seaman, John	WM	unk.	1890	10	Inmate	BMF
Sebrancke, Josh	WM	Feb.	1884	16	Janitor	44th
Seiling, Henry B.	WM	Nov.	1881	18	Lodger	44th
Seton, Eugene	WM	unk.	1890	10	Inmate	BMF
Shaefer, Chas.	WM	May	1882	18	Lodger	NWS
Shaorp, George	WM	unk.	1883	17	Inmate	BMF
Shea, James J.	WM	Sept.	1882	17	Lodger	NWS
Sheridan, Henry	WM	Jan.	1885	15	Inmate	WSB
Shields, Willie	WM	unk.	1891	9	Inmate	BMF
Siegel, Tony	WF	unk.	unk.	21	Inmate	EHG
Silleck, Emerson	WM	unk.	1891	9	Inmate	BMF
Silverman, Joseph	WM	July	1882	17	Inmate	BMF
Simmons, Thos.	WM	Apr.	1882	18	Lodger	NWS
Skinner, James	BM	Oct.	1884	15	Lodger	44th
Smith, Andrew	WM	Mar.	1884	16	Lodger	44th
Smith, Charles	WM	Apr.	1885	15	Inmate	WSB
Smith, Frederick	BM	Aug.	1883	16	Inmate	WSB
Smith, George	WM	Feb.	1881	19	Lodger	NWS
Smith, Grant	WM	Nov.	1866	33	Teamster	BMF
Smith, Harry	WM	Apr.	1883	17	Inmate	WSB
Smith, Harry	WM	Dec.	1881	18	Lodger	44th
Smith, Henry A.	WM	June	1882	17	Lodger	TMP
Smith, John J.	WM	Nov.	1882	17	Lodger	TMP
Smith, John	WM	Jan.	1882	18	Lodger	44th
Smith, John	WM	Mar.	1882	18	Lodger	NWS
Smith, Thomas	WM	June	1884	15	Lodger	TMP
Smith, William	WM	July	1885	14	Lodger	TMP
Smith, William	WM	Jun.	1882	18	Lodger	44th
Snyder, Charles	WM	unk.	1888	12	Inmate	BMF
Sockwood, Harry	WM	May	1881	19	Inmate	BMF
Steepelman, Morris	WM	July	1883	17	Inmate	WSB
Stephens, Agnes	WF	unk.	unk.	19	Inmate	EHG
Stisaro, James	WM	Oct.	1882	18	Inmate	WSB
Styres, Cora	WF	Sept.	1876	23	Servant	44th
Styres, Nora	WF	Nov.	1873	26	Servant	44th
Sullivan, Jermiah	WM	Oct.	1882	17	Lodger	NWS

Sullivan, Richard	WM	June	1876	23	Help	TMP
Thompson, James	WM	unk.	1892	8	Inmate	BMF
Thompson, Mamie	WF	unk.	unk.	16	Inmate	EHG
Thompson, Thomas	WM	unk.	1894	6	Inmate	BMF
Thorn, Thomas	BM	Mar.	1883	17	Inmate	WSB
Tice, Benj. W	WM	Oct.	1853	46	Superintendant	WSB
Tice, Clara L.	WF	May	1888	12	Daughter	WSB
Tice, Henry C.	WM	Oct.	1891	9	Son	WSB
Tice, Mary E.	WF	June	1847	53	Wife	WSB
Tice, Sarah M.	WF	May	1885	15	Daughter	WSB
Timka, John	WM	Sept.	1884	15	Lodger	44th
Trembles, Carl	WM	Nov.	1877	22	Teamster	BMF
Tully, James	WM	unk.	unk.	18	Inmate	WSB
Twombley, James	WM	Nov.	1881	18	Inmate	BMF
Umberant, Curt	WM	Apr.	1886	14	Inmate	BMF
Underwood, Bertha	WF	May	1877	23	Seamstress	BMF
Upright, Martha	WF	unk.	unk.	17	Inmate	EHG
Upright, Phoebe	WF	unk.	unk.	16	Inmate	EHG
Walker, Jonny	WM	Oct.	1882	17	Lodger	NWS
Wall, John	WM	Jan.	1882	18	Inmate	WSB
Wallace, Howard	WM	Oct.	1883	16	Inmate	WSB
Walsh, John N.	WM	Aug.	1882	17	Lodger	TMP
Walsh, Patrick	WM	Dec.	1881	18	Lodger	44th
Walton, Julia	WF	unk.	unk.	14	Inmate	EHG
Walz, William	WM	Dec.	1883	16	Lodger	NWS
Ward, Joseph	WM	July	1883	17	Inmate	WSB
Washburn, Florence	WF	unk.	unk.	17	Inmate	EHG
Water, Mark	WM	July	1883	16	Inmate	WSB
Watson, Albert	WM	Oct.	1882	17	Lodger	NWS
Weigert, William	WM	Jan.	1883	17	Lodger	44th
Weinberg, Louis	WM	May	1881	19	Lodger	NWS
Weinstein, Isadore	WM	unk.	1889	11	Inmate	BMF
Werner, Bartholomew A.	WM	Sept.	1879	20	Help	TMP
Whalen, Thomas	WM	Dec.	1883	16	Lodger	NWS
White, Charles	WM	Apr.	1883	17	Lodger	NWS
White, Charles	WM	Mar.	1884	16	Lodger	TMP
White, James	WM	Dec.	1886	13	Lodger	44th
White, James	WM	unk.	1890	10	Inmate	BMF
Whittaker, Mildred	WF	unk.	unk.	14	Inmate	EHG
Williams, John	WM	Feb.	1882	17	Inmate	WSB

Williams, Lizzie	WF	unk.	unk.	19	Inmate	EHG
Wilson, Thos.	WM	Nov.	1882	17	Lodger	NWS
Winn, Francis	WF	June	1871	28	Teacher	BMF
Woffard, Arthur	BM	Apr.	1884	16	Lodger	TMP
Wohlmocher, Willie	WM	unk.	1890	10	Inmate	BMF
Wood, Lillian	WF	Oct.	1872	27	Wife	44th
Wood, William	WM	Oct.	1873	26	Superintendant	44th
Wortendyke, John	WM	unk.	1860	40	-	BMF
Young, John	BM	Aug.	1887	12	Inmate	WSB
Young, Louis	WM	Jun.	1885	14	Lodger	TMP
Zeller, Fred	WM	Feb.	1884	16	Lodger	NWS

1905

Guide to Column Headings

in the

1905 New York State Enumeration

Name	Name of each person whose usual place of abode was in the institution on June 1, 1905. The census includes the name of every person living on June 1, 1905. Children born since June 1, 1905 were omitted. The surname is listed first, then the given name and middle initial.
R-G	Race and gender. "White" is designated by "W" and "Black" by "B". "Males are designated by "M" and females by "F".
*	Notes that the enumerator may have reported the information incorrectly.
A	Age at last birthday. Designated in years, unless otherwise noted with an "m" for "months". Generally, children who were less than one year old were described in terms of months.
Relation	Relationship of each person to the institution.

LH Lodging House. The following lodging houses were included in this census:

23rd: Temporary Home for Children
442 West 23rd Street
Assembly District 9, Election District 6

35th: West Side Lodging House
225 West 35th Street
Assembly District 11, Election District 16

44th: Forty-fourth Street Lodging House
247 East 44th Street
Assembly District 22, Election District 10

BMF: Brace Memorial Farm
Valhalla, Mount Pleasant,
Westchester County, Election District 4

EHG: Elizabeth Home for Girls
307 East 12th Street
Assembly District 14, Election District 4

EMS: Emergency Shelter for
Mothers with Children
311 East 12th Street
Assembly District 14, Election District 4

NWS: Newsboys' Lodging House
14 New Chambers Street
Assembly District 2, Election District 8

TMP: Tompkin's Square Lodging House
295 East 8th Street
Assembly District 14, Election District 17

Note Refer to the orginal census for the nativity, citizenship, and occupation of each person.

Name	R-G	A	Relation	LH
Ahring, Jessie	WF	16	Inmate	EHG
Albee, Abbie R.	WF	71	Seamstress	BMF
Alderman, Leon	WM	18	Lodger	NWS
Allen, Albert	WM	18	Lodger	44th
Allen, Annie	WF	15	Inmate	EHG
Allendorfer, Henry	WM	18	Boarder	35th
Anderson, Ella	WF	1	Boarder	23rd
Anderson, George	WM	18	Lodger	NWS
Anderson, John	WM	17	Lodger	NWS
Anderson, Thomas	WM	12	Inmate	BMF
Andrews, Charles	WM	16	Boarder	TMP
Anthony, Edward	WM	15	Inmate	BMF
Arthur, William	WM	11	Inmate	BMF
Ash, Albert	WM	27	Engineer	BMF
Ash, Grace, G.	WF	26	Assistant Matron	BMF
Barry, William	WM	19	Boarder	35th
Bash, Harry	WM	17	Lodger	NWS
Baus, Clara	WF	16	Inmate	EHG
Beade, Elizabeth	WF	1	Boarder	23rd
Becroft, Henry	WM	14	Lodger	44th
Behringer, Leo	WM	18	Lodger	44th
Beinstein, Hyman	WM	14	Lodger	NWS
Beltansky, David	WM	16	Lodger	NWS
Beny, Albert	WM	16	Lodger	NWS
Beranda, Charles	WM	18	Lodger	44th
Berg, Adolf	WM	18	Lodger	NWS
Berger, Samuel	WM	16	Lodger	44th
Bernet, Richard	BM	17	Lodger	44th
Berns, Louis	WM	16	Lodger	NWS
Beth-, Joseph	WM	17	Lodger	44th
Bethel, Michael	WM	15	Lodger	44th
Blank, Barney	WM	17	Lodger	NWS
Bloom, Isaac	WM	15	Boarder	TMP
Bloom, John	WM	15	Lodger	NWS
Bloomfield, Charles	WM	18	Lodger	NWS
Bogehold, Mary	WF	16	Inmate	EHG
Boilli, Andrew	WM	16	Lodger	NWS
Bondell, William	WM	10	Inmate	BMF
Borwer, Thomas	WM	16	Boarder	TMP

Bower, William	WM	19	Lodger	44th
Bradeley, Joseph	WM	18	Lodger	NWS
Bradsell, Eva	WF	65	Dining Room	BMF
Branse, Samuel	WM	14	Inmate	BMF
Brinehansky, Harry	WM	17	Lodger	NWS
Bristensten, Robert	WM	15	Inmate	BMF
Bristensten, William	WM	11	Inmate	BMF
Brown, Hattie	BF	7	Boarder	23rd
Brown, James	WM	21	Lodger	44th
Brown, John	WM	15	Lodger	NWS
Brown, John	WM	16	Lodger	NWS
Brown, John	WM	17	Boarder	35th
Brown, John	WM	18	Boarder	TMP
Brown, John	WM	19	Inmate	BMF
Brown, Louis	BM	15	Inmate	BMF
Brown, Thomas	WM	17	Lodger	44th
Buddenrick, Joseph	WM	15	Lodger	NWS
Bugbee, Ethel	WF	24	Dining Room	BMF
Bugbee, William W.	WM	58	Assistant Super.	BMF
Bugglen, Frederick	WM	18	Lodger	44th
Burke, John	WM	4	Boarder	23rd
Burke, Thomas	WM	18	Lodger	NWS
Burns, Joseph	WM	17	Lodger	NWS
Burns, Patrick	WM	16	Lodger	44th
Burns, William	WM	15	Lodger	44th
Burny, Joseph	WM	16	Lodger	44th
Burris, Louis S.	WM	25	Caretaker	BMF
Bush, Harry	WM	17	Inmate	BMF
Bush, Paul	WM	18	Lodger	NWS
Butler, James	WM	18	Lodger	NWS
Cahill, Thomas	WM	22	Lodger	NWS
Callahan, John	WM	17	Lodger	44th
Callghan, Patrick	WM	16	Boarder	TMP
Campbell, James	WM	16	Boarder	TMP
Carey, Peter	WM	14	Boarder	35th
Carroll, William	WM	16	Inmate	BMF
Carter, George	WM	17	Lodger	NWS
Case, George	WM	16	Boarder	TMP
Casey, Charles	WM	18	Lodger	NWS
Casey, Patrick	WM	16	Boarder	TMP
Casino, Albert	WM	16	Boarder	TMP

Castagnor, Tony	WM	16	Inmate	BMF
Ceverny, John	WM	18	Lodger	44th
Chambers, Edward	WM	16	Lodger	44th
Childs, Arthur	WM	17	Boarder	TMP
Cigil, Max	WM	19	Boarder	TMP
Clancy, James J.	WM	28	Boarder	TMP
Clancy, Mary R.	WF	35	Boarder	TMP
Clancy, William	WM	21	Boarder	TMP
Clark, Helen	WF	16	Inmate	EHG
Clark, John	WM	17	Inmate	BMF
Clark, Thomas	WM	16	Boarder	TMP
Claus, James	WM	18	Lodger	NWS
Cleveland, William	WM	21	Janitor	44th
Cline, Alta M.	WF	28	Matron	BMF
Cline, Carry W.	WM	27	Farmer	BMF
Clinton, Stephen	WM	17	Boarder	TMP
Cochrane, Samuel	WM	18	Lodger	44th
Codey, John	WM	18	Boarder	TMP
Coffee, Charles	WM	18	Lodger	44th
Coghlan, Daniel	WM	18	Lodger	NWS
Cohen, Abe	WM	18	Lodger	NWS
Cohen, Charles	WM	18	Lodger	NWS
Cohen, Isidore	WM	18	Lodger	NWS
Colby, George	WM	28	Son	ESW
Colby, Julia G.	WF	40	Matron	ESW
Coleman, Lizzie	WF	14	Inmate	EHG
Coles, Earl	BM	12	Inmate	BMF
Collins, James	WM	16	Boarder	35th
Collins, John	WM	17	Boarder	TMP
Comstock, Blanch	WF	23	Cook	BMF
Comstock, Clara B.	WF	25	Teacher	BMF
Comstock, David	WM	24	Farmer	BMF
Conclauder, Jennie	WF	28	Inmate	EHG
Conelly, Estelle	WF	14	Inmate	EHG
Conklin, Hattie	WF	14	Inmate	EHG
Connelly, James	WM	17	Boarder	35th
Connors, Richard	WM	35	Night Clerk	44th
Cook, Earl	WM	12	Inmate	BMF
Cook, Joseph	WM	17	Lodger	NWS
Corkdale, Jeanette	WF	14	Inmate	EHG
Cothalaer, Joseph	WM	7	Inmate	BMF

Courtright, Floyd R.	WM	38	Boarder	TMP
Covell, Dora	WF	53	Superintendant	23rd
Cowans, James	WM	16	Lodger	NWS
Cragen, Paterick	WM	18	Lodger	NWS
Cuelyn, Jean	WM	18	Lodger	NWS
Cuff, Delia	WF	40	Inmate	EHG
Cunningham, Wm.	WM	17	Lodger	NWS
Curley, John J.	WM	18	Lodger	44th
Curley, William	WM	18	Lodger	NWS
Cusherter, Clyde	WM	13	Inmate	BMF
Cushner, James	WM	18	Boarder	35th
Daigler, Elvin	WM	16	Lodger	44th
Dale, Joseph	WM	17	Lodger	NWS
Daley, Peter	WM	18	Lodger	NWS
Daly, Emmet	WM	18	Lodger	44th
Daly, Frank	WM	18	Boarder	35th
Daly, John	WM	16	Inmate	BMF
Daly, William	WM	16	Lodger	44th
Darling, Elizabeth J.	WF	31	Cook	BMF
Darling, George W.	WM	29	Night Watchman	BMF
Dean, Walter	WM	18	Lodger	NWS
Deans, Thomas	WM	18	Lodger	NWS
Deen, Edward	WM	19	Lodger	44th
DeHope, William	WM	11	Inmate	BMF
Delong, David	WM	18	Lodger	44th
Dempsey, John	WM	17	Lodger	NWS
Denney, James	WM	18	Lodger	NWS
Denning, William	WM	17	Lodger	44th
Dillen, Matthew	WM	14	Lodger	NWS
Donald, John	WM	16	Lodger	NWS
Dow, John	WM	18	Inmate	BMF
Downes, Mary	WF	45	Laundress	EHG
Doyle, Joseph	WM	16	Lodger	44th
Driscoll, Frank	WM	16	Lodger	44th
Driscoll, James	WM	18	Boarder	35th
Duffy, Charles	WM	17	Lodger	NWS
Dundon, James	WM	17	Inmate	BMF
Dunn, James	WM	17	Boarder	35th
Dunn, John	WM	18	Boarder	35th
Eagleson, Alice	WF	8	Boarder	23rd
Eagleson, Hellen	WF	2	Boarder	23rd

Eagleson, Mary	WF	5	Boarder	23rd
Effias, Sam	WM	16	Lodger	NWS
Egan, Matthew	WM	18	Boarder	TMP
Ehrlich, Max	WM	16	Boarder	TMP
Elsworth, Marie	WF	14	Inmate	EHG
Entwistle, Joseph	WM	18	Lodger	NWS
Eskowitz, Samuel	WM	18	Boarder	TMP
Evans, Frank	BM	15	Boarder	35th
Evans, Harry	WM	15	Inmate	BMF
Fade, Alfred	BM	16	Boarder	35th
Fagan, John	WM	16	Lodger	44th
Farrell, James	WM	18	Lodger	NWS
Farrington, George	WM	16	Boarder	TMP
Farrington, George	WM	16	Boarder	35th
Fasselli, James	WM	18	Lodger	NWS
Feeley, Paterick	WM	18	Lodger	NWS
Feinberg, Philip	WM	17	Lodger	NWS
Feldman, Max	WM	6	Inmate	BMF
Fenen, William	WM	17	Lodger	NWS
Festnit, Emil	WM	17	Inmate	BMF
Fickert, Alma	WF	16	Inmate	EHG
Finges, Alexander	WM	16	Lodger	NWS
Finkelstin, Mathew	WM	17	Lodger	44th
Finn, Joseph	WM	16	Lodger	44th
Finnigan, Joseph	WM	15	Lodger	44th
Fischer, Hyman	WM	15	Lodger	NWS
Fish, Abraham	WM	16	Boarder	TMP
Fisher, Monroe	WM	18	Boarder	TMP
Fitzpatrick, Patrick J.	WM	17	Lodger	44th
Flanagan, Charles	WM	18	Lodger	NWS
Flanagan, Geo.	WM	18	Lodger	NWS
Flanagan, John	WM	18	Lodger	NWS
Flanigan, Bernard	WM	15	Lodger	44th
Fott, Katie	WF	16	Inmate	EHG
Fox, Harry	WM	16	Inmate	BMF
Free, Michael	WM	17	Boarder	35th
Freedman, Louis	WM	15	Lodger	NWS
Fritz, Henry	WM	14	Inmate	BMF
Fuch, Joseph	WM	15	Lodger	NWS
Funell, William	WM	14	Lodger	NWS
Fungs, Alexander	WM	16	Inmate	BMF

Futterer, Henry	WM	16	Boarder	35th
Gaber, Morris	WM	17	Boarder	TMP
Ganzon, Frank	WM	15	Boarder	35th
Gast, Samuel	WM	16	Boarder	TMP
Gauve, Louis	WM	17	Boarder	35th
Gerald, Arlisonn	WM	16	Inmate	BMF
Gerald, Nathan	WM	19	Boarder	35th
Geraty, Joseph	WM	18	Lodger	44th
Gesel, Rudolf	WM	17	Inmate	BMF
Gibbs, James	BM	17	Boarder	35th
Gibson, Nathan	WM	18	Lodger	NWS
Gibson, William	WM	18	Lodger	NWS
Gilbret, Philip	WM	14	Inmate	BMF
Gillen, James	WM	16	Boarder	35th
Gillery, John	WM	16	Boarder	TMP
Gilroy, Edward	WM	18	Lodger	44th
Ginz, David	WM	16	Inmate	BMF
Goff, Clarc L.	WM	11	At School	BMF
Goff, Eva M.	WF	45	Matron	BMF
Goff, Floyd G.	WM	45	Superintendant	BMF
Goff, Ginie	WF	36	Laundress	BMF
Goff, Martin H.	WM	47	Farm Foreman	BMF
Goldberg, Harrry	WM	16	Boarder	TMP
Goldberg, Solomon	WM	15	Lodger	NWS
Goldner, Fred	WM	15	Lodger	NWS
Goodman, Max	WM	15	Boarder	TMP
Goodman, Morris	WM	18	Boarder	TMP
Green, Charles	WM	18	Inmate	BMF
Green, Robert	WM	18	Boarder	35th
Green, William	WM	17	Lodger	44th
Greene, William	WM	17	Boarder	TMP
Griffin, Frank	WM	18	Lodger	NWS
Gross, John	WM	18	Lodger	NWS
Gross, Samuel	WM	17	Boarder	TMP
Hains, Alfred	WM	15	Lodger	NWS
Hall, John E.	WM	17	Lodger	NWS
Halloran, Bert	WM	17	Lodger	NWS
Hamilton, Helen	WF	15	Inmate	EHG
Hanar, May	WF	29	Nurse	23rd
Hanis, Sam	WM	18	Lodger	NWS
Hannigan, Joseph	WM	18	Lodger	NWS

Hannigan, Thomas	WM	18	Lodger	44th
Harrison, Benjamin	WM	16	Boarder	TMP
Hartung, August	WM	18	Boarder	35th
Hartwell, William	WM	17	Boarder	TMP
Haynes, Lizzie	WF	14	Inmate	EHG
Healey, Thomas	WM	18	Lodger	NWS
Hefferman, Charles	WM	18	Lodger	NWS
Heig, Andrew	WM	15	Son	NWS
Heig, Anna	WF	11	Daughter	NWS
Heig, Margaret	WF	13	Daughter	NWS
Heig, Mrs. Rudolph	WF	42	Ass't. Super.	NWS
Heig, Oscar	WM	16	Son	NWS
Heig, Rudolph	WM	41	Superintendant	NWS
Hennan, Carl	WM	18	Lodger	NWS
Herrera, Mary	WF	14	Inmate	EHG
Herron, Henry	WM	18	Lodger	NWS
Hessel, Henry	WM	17	Lodger	44th
Hodgins, Thomas	WM	18	Lodger	NWS
Holman, Peter	WM	17	Boarder	35th
Holmbeck, Frank	WM	17	Boarder	35th
Holmes, Felix	WM	18	Lodger	NWS
Hubion, Morris	WM	17	Boarder	TMP
Huces, Marie	WF	40	Caretaker	EHG
Hudson, Henry G.	WM	38	Boarder	35th
Hudson, Jessie	WF	22	Cook	44th
Humar, Harry	WM	16	Boarder	TMP
Hunt, Fletcher	WM	15	Lodger	NWS
Hurley, Elizabeth	WF	60	Matron	EHG
Hussy, James	WM	16	Inmate	BMF
Ingliss, August	WM	16	Lodger	44th
Jacobs, Louise	WF	13	Inmate	EHG
Jacobson, Chas.	WM	18	Lodger	NWS
Jacobson, Harry	WM	19	Boarder	TMP
Jacoby, Frank	WM	15	Lodger	44th
Jaffe, Julius	WM	16	Lodger	NWS
Jaffe, Sam	WM	14	Lodger	NWS
Jahle, Valentine	WM	18	Lodger	44th
Jahrling, William	WM	16	Boarder	35th
Jenks, Charles	WM	17	Inmate	BMF
Jenks, Clement	WM	5	Inmate	BMF
Jennings, Thomas	WM	17	Boarder	35th

Jennings, William	WM	18	Boarder	35th
Jensen, Henry	WM	18	Lodger	44th
Johnson, Peter	WM	18	Lodger	44th
Johnston, Annie	WF	22	Inmate	EHG
Jones, Magaret	WF	14	Inmate	EHG
Jordan, James	BM	20	Boarder	35th
Josephurtz, Jacob	WM	18	Boarder	TMP
Jsrail, Lion	WM	19	Boarder	TMP
Kahe, Louis	WM	18	Boarder	TMP
Kamross, Daniel	WM	13	Boarder	35th
Kane, James	WM	18	Lodger	NWS
Katz, Abe	WM	15	Lodger	NWS
Keenan, Charles	WM	17	Lodger	44th
Kelly, John	WM	15	Boarder	TMP
Kelly, John	WM	18	Lodger	NWS
Kennedy, James	WM	16	Boarder	35th
Kenney, Harry	WM	16	Inmate	BMF
Kenyon, Arthur C.	WM	60	Superintendant	TMP
Kenyon, Henry	WM	19	Son	TMP
Kenyon, Lottie C.	WF	55	Wife	TMP
Keppers, Isaac	WM	14	Lodger	NWS
Kersten, Edard	WM	18	Lodger	44th
Killieren, Marian	WF	12	Inmate	EHG
King, John	WM	17	Boarder	35th
Kingsland, Harry	WM	12	Inmate	BMF
Klein, Bernard	WM	15	Boarder	35th
Klein, Sarah	WF	13	Inmate	EHG
Koppel, Ernest	WM	15	Inmate	BMF
Krietz, Charles	WM	18	Boarder	TMP
Krone, Samuel	WM	18	Lodger	NWS
Krugh, Oswald	WM	15	Lodger	44th
Kurtz, Chas.	WM	14	Lodger	NWS
Kurtz, Harry	WM	14	Lodger	NWS
Lake, Henry	WM	18	Lodger	44th
Lamb, Christopher	WM	18	Lodger	NWS
Lannon, Robert	WM	17	Inmate	BMF
Larchevegue, Henry	WM	18	Boarder	35th
Larkin, John	WM	14	Lodger	44th
Larkin, Joseph	WM	13	Lodger	44th
LaRotunda, Rose	WF	14	Inmate	EHG
Leary, Mary	WF	26	Chambermaid	44th

Lebowitz, Herman	WM	13	Boarder	35th
Ledderet, Abraham	WM	16	Boarder	TMP
Ledderet, Morris	WM	17	Boarder	TMP
Lefevre, Michael	WM	16	Boarder	35th
Leonard, Joseph	WM	17	Boarder	TMP
Leower, Lewis	WM	16	Lodger	NWS
Lepini, Filian	WF	18	Inmate	EHG
Levene, Max	WM	16	Boarder	TMP
Levin, Morris	WM	16	Lodger	NWS
Levy, Morris	WM	17	Boarder	TMP
Levy, Samuel	WM	14	Lodger	NWS
Lewis, Benjamin	WM	18	Boarder	TMP
Lewis, Morris	WM	15	Lodger	NWS
Lichtman, Benjamin	WM	17	Lodger	44th
Linden, Israel	WM	17	Lodger	NWS
Link, Jacob	WM	18	Lodger	NWS
Littlebaum, Oscar	WM	16	Boarder	TMP
Louvey, Frank	WM	16	Lodger	NWS
Ludderman, Laz.	WM	16	Lodger	NWS
Lutroni, Santo	WM	16	Lodger	NWS
Lynch, John	WM	18	Lodger	NWS
Lyons, Frank	WM	16	Lodger	44th
Lyons, William	WM	18	Lodger	44th
Maine, Nellie	WF	13	Inmate	EHG
Major, Harry	WM	15	Lodger	NWS
Makes, Edward	WM	16	Lodger	NWS
Mansser, George	WM	18	Lodger	NWS
Marchinio, Daniel	WM	17	Boarder	35th
Martin, Mary	WF	60	Boarder	35th
Mayers, Joseph	WM	17	Lodger	44th
McArthur, George	WM	18	Lodger	44th
McCabe, James	WM	18	Lodger	NWS
McCannon, John	WM	15	Lodger	NWS
McCarthy, Richard	WM	18	Lodger	44th
McClain, William	WM	15	Lodger	NWS
McConnor, John	WM	17	Inmate	BMF
McCounack, Ethon	WM	17	Lodger	NWS
McCreif, Charles	WM	18	Boarder	35th
McCurdy, Joseph	WM	18	Lodger	NWS
McDevett, John	WM	17	Lodger	NWS
McDonald, Arthur	WM	18	Lodger	NWS

McDonald, Geo.	WM	15	Lodger	NWS
McDonald, John	WM	16	Lodger	NWS
McDonald, Thomas	WM	17	Lodger	44th
McFetridge, William	WM	9	Inmate	BMF
McGarry, William	WM	7	Inmate	BMF
McGough, James	WM	17	Lodger	44th
McGovern, James	WM	16	Lodger	44th
McGrath, Michael	WM	18	Lodger	44th
McGuire, James	WM	18	Lodger	44th
McGusham, Herb.	WM	17	Lodger	NWS
McKee, Anna	WF	17	Inmate	EHG
McKee, Mary	WF	32	Wife	35th
McKee, William C.	WM	35	Superintendant	35th
McKibbin, Hannah R.	WF	54	Seamstress	BMF
McMann, James	WM	18	Boarder	TMP
McName, Henry	WM	18	Boarder	TMP
McNeal, George	WM	17	Lodger	NWS
Mebrant, John	WM	18	Boarder	TMP
Meehan, John	WM	19	Lodger	NWS
Meehan, Joseph	WM	18	Lodger	NWS
Mellen, John	WM	15	Lodger	44th
Mendez, Monellino	WM	18	Lodger	NWS
Mericle, Frank	WM	29	Boarder	TMP
Metschios, Louis	WM	18	Lodger	NWS
Meyers, John	WM	16	Inmate	BMF
Mikoda, Johanna	WF	18	Lodger	NWS
Miller, Charles	WM	18	Boarder	35th
Miller, Michael	WM	14	Boarder	35th
Millerstein, Geo.	WM	16	Lodger	NWS
Milstein, Louis	WM	16	Boarder	TMP
Mirtzer, William	WM	8	Inmate	BMF
Mollinose, Mich.	WM	16	Lodger	NWS
Montgomery, John H.	WM	17	Boarder	TMP
Morrisey, Wm.	WM	18	Lodger	NWS
Morrison, John	WM	16	Lodger	44th
Morrow, Sadie	WF	18	Inmate	EHG
Moses, Abraham	WM	15	Inmate	BMF
Moses, Rudolf	WM	12	Inmate	BMF
Mukele, Sam	WM	18	Lodger	NWS
Mulhearn, Edw.	WM	23	Lodger	NWS
Mullen, Michale	WM	17	Lodger	44th

Murphy, James	WM	18	Lodger	NWS
Murray, Aurthur	WM	16	Lodger	NWS
Murry, Thomas	WM	13	Inmate	BMF
Nagle, David	WM	16	Lodger	44th
Nash, Edward	WM	13	Lodger	NWS
Nash, William	WM	11	Lodger	NWS
Nelson, Charles	WM	15	Inmate	BMF
Nelson, Thomas	WM	16	Lodger	NWS
Newman, William	WM	17	Lodger	44th
Noble, John	WM	18	Lodger	NWS
Nolan, Mary	WF	35	Kitchen-maid	44th
Nolan, Timothy	WM	17	Lodger	44th
Nussbaum, George	WM	16	Boarder	TMP
Nusted, Samuel	WM	18	Boarder	TMP
O'Connell, Thomas	WM	18	Lodger	NWS
Odell, Michael	WM	17	Boarder	35th
Oliver, Claude	WM	17	Lodger	NWS
Olsen, George	WM	17	Boarder	TMP
O'Meara, David	WM	16	Lodger	NWS
Orvitz, Max	WM	16	Lodger	NWS
Oserin, William	WM	17	Lodger	NWS
Otte, Bertha	WF	25	Laundress	EHG
Parker, Elizabeth	WF	45	Ass't. Matron	EHG
Parsons, Anna	WF	27	Nurse	23rd
Pauli, Frank	WM	17	Lodger	NWS
Pearson, Herbert	WM	18	Lodger	NWS
Peck, Florence	WF	19	Boarder	23rd
Pelletrie, Antonett	WF	18	Laundress	EHG
Pendleton, William	WM	16	Lodger	44th
Phalen, William	WM	18	Lodger	NWS
Phillips, Henry	WM	16	Lodger	44th
Pierson, John	WM	19	Boarder	TMP
Pincus, Isidor	WM	15	Boarder	TMP
Pinkman, James	WM	21	Lodger	NWS
Pinus, Lawrence	WM	17	Boarder	35th
Pocillo, Joseph	WM	16	Lodger	NWS
Post, Gertrude	WF	22	Inmate	EHG
Prise, Delia	WF	8	Boarder	23rd
Quinn, Annie	WF	23	Inmate	EHG
Rabelle, Frieda	WF	16	Inmate	EHG
Rabinowitz, Harry	WM	16	Lodger	NWS

Reed, Andrew	WM	16	Inmate	BMF
Resse, Maria	WF	24	Inmate	EHG
Retting, Frederick	WM	17	Lodger	44th
Reynolds, Harry	WM	15	Lodger	NWS
Reynolds, James	WM	15	Lodger	NWS
Rice, George	WM	17	Boarder	35th
Rice, Thomas	WM	17	Boarder	TMP
Richards, Lizzie	WF	15	Inmate	EHG
Ring, Richard	WM	17	Boarder	35th
Rob, Ellias	WM	16	Lodger	NWS
Robinson, Woverly	WM	18	Lodger	NWS
Roe, Mary	WF	17	Inmate	EHG
Rogers, George	WM	16	Inmate	BMF
Rogers, George	WM	16	Lodger	44th
Ronan, Timothy	WM	22	Caretaker	BMF
Rooney, James	WM	16	Inmate	BMF
Rooney, James	WM	17	Lodger	NWS
Rooney, Quigley	WM	15	Boarder	35th
Rose, Charles	WM	18	Lodger	44th
Rose, James	WM	16	Lodger	NWS
Rubin, George	WM	16	Lodger	NWS
Ruggiero, Louis	WM	18	Lodger	44th
Russell, Lilian	WF	14	Inmate	EHG
Ruth, David	WM	19	Boarder	TMP
Ryan, Joseph	WM	18	Lodger	NWS
Scanlell, Julia	WF	40	Inmate	EHG
Scanlon, Robert	WM	18	Lodger	NWS
Schafer, Harry	WM	17	Lodger	NWS
Scheer, Tony	WM	16	Inmate	BMF
Scheer, Tony	WM	16	Lodger	NWS
Schneider, Chas.	WM	14	Lodger	NWS
Schneider, Morris	WM	18	Lodger	NWS
Schoner, Michael	WM	16	Inmate	BMF
Schoor, Charles	WM	18	Boarder	35th
Schradel, Michael	WM	17	Lodger	44th
Schroder, Robert	WM	15	Inmate	BMF
Schultz, Frank	WM	17	Lodger	NWS
Seamans, George	WM	17	Lodger	NWS
Seely, Gertrude	WF	25	Inmate	EHG
Sengler, Benjamin	WM	16	Boarder	TMP
Shepard, George	WM	17	Lodger	NWS

Shepley, Laura P.	WF	66	Mother-In-Law	35th
Sheridan, John	WM	16	Inmate	BMF
Siegel, Antonia	WF	19	Inmate	EHG
Sigmon, William	WM	12	Inmate	BMF
Silestro, Angelo	WM	14	Lodger	NWS
Silverman, Isaac	WM	16	Lodger	NWS
Silverstein, Benjamin	WM	19	Boarder	TMP
Simpson, Wayne	WM	17	Lodger	NWS
Skelly, Philip	WM	15	Lodger	44th
Smallwood, Oliver	BM	18	Boarder	35th
Smith, Anthony	WM	17	Lodger	NWS
Smith, Charles	CM	16	Lodger	44th
Smith, Edward	WM	9	Inmate	BMF
Smith, Herbert	WM	15	Inmate	BMF
Smith, Ida	WF	14	Inmate	EHG
Smith, Joseph	WM	18	Boarder	TMP
Smith, Joseph	WM	18	Lodger	NWS
Smith, Katie	WF	16	Inmate	EHG
Smith, William	WM	17	Lodger	NWS
Specht, Frieda	WF	25	Inmate	EHG
Spillane, Daniel	WM	16	Lodger	44th
Spitzer, Charles	WM	18	Boarder	TMP
Stahle, Louis	WM	16	Inmate	BMF
Stark, Samuel	WM	15	Lodger	NWS
Stein, Charles	WM	16	Inmate	BMF
Steinberg, Harry	WM	15	Lodger	NWS
Stern, Joseph	WM	17	Lodger	NWS
Stevens, Harry	WM	17	Lodger	NWS
Stillman, William	WM	13	Lodger	NWS
Strand, Chester	WM	17	Lodger	NWS
Strong, Richard	WM	17	Boarder	TMP
Strut, Otto	WM	16	Lodger	44th
Sullivan, Daniel	WM	18	Lodger	44th
Sullivan, Hanna	WF	25	Cook	EHG
Sullivan, John	WM	17	Inmate	BMF
Sullivan, John	WM	17	Lodger	44th
Sullivan, John	WM	18	Lodger	44th
Sullivan, Nora	WF	38	Lodger	NWS
Swykenburgh, Andrew	WM	12	Inmate	BMF
Taylor, Nellie	WF	15	Inmate	EHG
Thering, Annie	WF	14	Inmate	EHG

Thompson, Mary	WF	30	Inmate	EHG
Tordriff, Emil	WM	16	Lodger	44th
Troonsegand, Geo.	WM	16	Lodger	NWS
Twoney, Timo.	WM	18	Lodger	NWS
Ule, George	WM	14	Inmate	BMF
Ule, Walter	WM	9	Inmate	BMF
VanCott, Marian	WF	45	Housekeeper	EHG
Vandervortt, Charles	WM	11	Boarder	TMP
Vandervortt, Louis	WM	15	Boarder	TMP
Victoria, Michel	WM	18	Lodger	44th
Voght, August	WM	18	Lodger	44th
Wallach, Henry	WM	16	Lodger	44th
Walsh, John	WM	16	Lodger	NWS
Walsh, John	WM	18	Boarder	TMP
Walsh, John	WM	18	Lodger	NWS
Walsh, Maurice	WM	16	Lodger	44th
Walsh, William	WM	18	Lodger	NWS
Wampole, Fred	WM	17	Lodger	NWS
Ward, John	WM	17	Lodger	NWS
Warde, Frank	WM	16	Lodger	NWS
Washburn, Florence	WF	19	Inmate	EHG
Washington, George	CM	18	Lodger	44th
Waynetaka, John	WM	16	Lodger	44th
Weber, John	WM	18	Lodger	NWS
Weber, Walter	WM	16	Boarder	TMP
Weil, George	WM	11	Inmate	BMF
Weil, Herman	WM	14	Inmate	BMF
Weinberg, Abraham	WM	15	Boarder	TMP
Weisenbaum, Benjamin	WM	16	Boarder	TMP
Welsh, William	WM	17	Boarder	35th
Wetmoore, Marie	WF	25	Boarder	ESW
Wetmoore, May	WF	21	Boarder	ESW
Wexler, Jacob	WM	16	Lodger	NWS
White, Charles	WM	17	Boarder	TMP
White, Frank	WM	18	Lodger	44th
White, James	WM	12	Inmate	BMF
Wiener, Abe	WM	15	Lodger	NWS
Wilkins, Lula E.	WF	19	Dining Room	BMF
Willette, Dorman	WM	18	Lodger	NWS
Williams, Frank	WM	16	Lodger	44th
Williams, Frank	WM	17	Lodger	NWS

Williams, Henry	WM	16	Lodger	44th
Williams, Jacob	WM	16	Lodger	NWS
Williams, Jacob	WM	17	Lodger	NWS
Williams, Joseph	WM	16	Inmate	BMF
Williams, Lizzie	WF	24	Inmate	EHG
Wilson, John	WM	16	Lodger	NWS
Wingerter, Maria	WF	37	Boarder	23rd
Wingerter, Richard	WM	7	Boarder	23rd
Winkle, Thomas	WM	18	Lodger	44th
Winters, John	WM	18	Boarder	35th
Wixon, Beatrice	WF	7	Boarder	23rd
Wolkers, Walter	WM	17	Lodger	NWS
Wood, Lillian	WF	32	Wife	44th
Wood, William	WM	31	Superintendant	44th
Yamagata, Flognet	WM	12	Inmate	BMF
Yamagata, Harry	WM	11	Inmate	BMF
Young, Joseph	WM	16	Lodger	44th

1910

Guide to Column Headings

in the

1910 Federal Enumeration

Name Name of each person whose usual place of abode was in the institution on April 15, 1910. The census includes the name of every person living on April 15, 1910. Children born since April 15, 1910 were omitted. The surname is listed first, then the given name and middle initial.

R-G Race and gender. "White" is designated by "W" and "Black"by "B". Males are designated by "M" and "Females" by "F".

* Notes that the enumerator may have reported the name or gender incorrectly.

A Age at last birthday. Designated in years, unless otherwise noted with an "m" for "months".

Relation Relationship of each person to the institution.

LH Lodging House. The following lodging houses were included in this census:

35th: West Side Boys' Lodging House
225 West 35th
Enumeration District 1194

44th: Forty-fourth Street Lodging House
247 East 44th Street
Enumeration District 1106

BMF: Brace Memorial Farm
Valhalla, Mount Pleasant,
Westchester County
Enumeration District 51

EHG: Elizabeth Home for Girls
307 East 12th Street
Enumeration District 1078

ESW: Emergency Shelter for
Mothers with Children
311 East 12th Street
Enumeration District 1078

HBH: Harlem Boys' Hotel
136 East 127th Street
Enumeration District 424

NWS: Newsboys' Lodging House
14 New Chambers Street
Enumeration District 14

TMP: Tompkin's Square Lodging House
295 East 8th Street
Enumeration District 1669

Note — Refer to the orginal census for the nativity, birthplace, language, and occupation of each resident.

Name	R-G	A	Relation	LH
Alanagan, George H.	WM	20	Lodger	NWS
Allen, James	WM	19	Lodger	NWS
Anderson, Margaret	WF	15	Lodger	EHG
Angelo, John	WM	17	Lodger	44th
Anstly, Frank	WM	17	Lodger	44th
Arnold, Glaney	WM	16	Lodger	NWS
Ast, Joseph	WM	16	Inmate	TMP
Augur, Frank J.	WM	18	Lodger	NWS
Averill, Allyn A.	WM	18	Lodger	NWS
Backly, Willford	WM	17	Lodger	NWS
Baduer, Edward	WM	17	Inmate	TMP
Bailey, James	WM	18	Lodger	HBH
Baker, Bertha	WF	36	Servant	BMF
Baker, Edward	WM	16	Inmate	BMF
Baker, George	WM	16	Son	BMF
Baker, Herman	WM	40	Farm Laborer	BMF
Barlew, Rita	WF	19	Lodger	EHG
Barn, Wilfred	WM	18	Inmate	BMF
Barnshaw, Thomas	WM	15	Lodger	35th
Bartels, Charles	WM	17	Lodger	44th
Bauer, William	WM	25	Janitor	44th
Baumstone, Morris	WM	18	Lodger	44th
Beck, Joseph	WM	18	Lodger	35th
Beeching, Celia A.	WF	69	Lodger	EHG
Been, Mary	WF	14	Lodger	EHG
Beeser, Harry	WM	15	Lodger	NWS
Belley, Mozareh	WM	44	Cook	35th
Belmar, Herbert	WM	18	Lodger	44th
Bender, Albert W.	WM	31	Hired Man	BMF
Bennett, Nellie	WF	24	Teacher	BMF
Berg, Max	WM	18	Lodger	HBH
Berger, Harry	WM	17	Lodger	NWS
Berger, Joseph	WM	17	Inmate	TMP
Berry, William	WM	17	Lodger	35th
Bertram, Laurence J.	WM	18	Lodger	NWS
Best, Edward	WM	10	Son	BMF
Best, Edward	WM	11	Inmate	BMF
Best, Sarah	WF	45	Servant	BMF
Binder, Oliver	WM	16	Inmate	BMF

Blakie, Robert	WM	19	Lodger	NWS
Bleakley, Isabella	WM*	29	Servant	HBH
Blohm, Walter	WM	16	Lodger	NWS
Blum, Hyman	WM	18	Inmate	TMP
Boden, August	WM	22	Lodger	HBH
Boden, Fred	WM	16	Lodger	HBH
Bollenbach, John	WM	19	Inmate	BMF
Bomgeinent, William	WM	17	Inmate	BMF
Borden, Henry H.	WM	18	Inmate	BMF
Borstein, Morris	WM	17	Inmate	TMP
Boyd, William	BM	17	Inmate	TMP
Boyer, Don.	WM	18	Lodger	35th
Boyle, Daniel	WM	18	Inmate	BMF
Brace, Leon	WM	19	Inmate	BMF
Brady, James	WM	17	Inmate	BMF
Brady, James	WM	18	Inmate	TMP
Brahms, Lanida	WF	18	Lodger	EHG
Braverman, Abe	WM	17	Lodger	HBH
Breen, Thomas F.	WM	18	Lodger	NWS
Brennan, James	WM	17	Lodger	44th
Brigam, Charles	WM	15	Inmate	BMF
Broun, Cara	WF	25	Lodger	EHG
Brown, Charles	WM	17	Lodger	44th
Brown, James	WM	18	Lodger	44th
Bryan, George	WM	16	Lodger	HBH
Buck, Howard	WM	11	Inmate	BMF
Budd, Richard	BM	18	Inmate	TMP
Burke, Deneer D.	WM	18	Lodger	NWS
Burke, John D.	WM	15	Lodger	35th
Burke, Joseph	WM	18	Lodger	NWS
Burns, Albert	WM	18	Lodger	35th
Butler, Louis	WM	9	Inmate	BMF
Byrnes, John J.	WM	18	Lodger	NWS
Cahill, John J.	WM	18	Lodger	NWS
Callahan, Joseph E.	WM	16	Lodger	NWS
Calser, David H.	WM	15	Lodger	NWS
Caps, Antonio	WM	17	Lodger	35th
Carlon, Edward	WM	17	Inmate	BMF
Carr, Howard J.	WM	17	Lodger	44th
Carroll, Joseph	WM	16	Lodger	35th
Carsen, Edwin A.	WM	16	Lodger	NWS

Carter, John	WM	17	Lodger	44th
Carvasstey, Minnie	WF	18	Lodger	EHG
Cassia, Michael	WM	14	Inmate	BMF
Caulfield, Bessie	WF	22	Inmate	ESW
Caulfield, John	WM	0m	Inmate	ESW
Causblein, David I.	WM	19	Lodger	NWS
Cerroth, Anthony	WM	11	Inmate	BMF
Chambers, Clara	WF	16	Lodger	EHG
Chapman, John	WM	18	Lodger	44th
Cheffers, Joseph W.	WM	49	Janitor	35th
Chiming, Joseph	WM	16	Inmate	TMP
Cleacy, James R.	WM	24	Lodger	NWS
Coff, Delia	WF	58	Lodger	EHG
Coffery, Joseph	WM	16	Lodger	HBH
Coffy, Katie	WF	35	Cook	TMP
Coggswell, Anna	WF	17	Lodger	EHG
Cohen, Are	WF	16	Lodger	EHG
Cohen, Max	WM	16	Lodger	44th
Colby, George Z.	WM	32	Son	ESW
Colby, Julia G.	WF	56	Matron	ESW
Coleman, James	WM	19	Lodger	44th
Collin, Annie	WF	26	Lodger	EHG
Comstock, Clara	WF	30	Servant	BMF
Connolly, Phillip	WM	18	Lodger	HBH
Connors, Richard Andrew	WM	37	Lodger	44th
Cook, Harry	WM	14	Inmate	BMF
Cooperstein, Joseph	WM	18	Lodger	NWS
Corbett, Elsie	WF	16	Lodger	EHG
Cortes, Andrew	WM	16	Lodger	44th
Cortes, Andrew	WM	17	Lodger	44th
Costello, Chas. J.	WM	19	Lodger	NWS
Cottrull, William	WM	14	Lodger	HBH
Cox, Thomas	WM	20	Inmate	BMF
Coyle, Owen	WM	17	Lodger	44th
Crank, Clarence R.	WM	16	Lodger	NWS
Crispo, Albert	WM	18	Lodger	HBH
Crowe, Thomas	WM	18	Inmate	TMP
Crowley, John	WM	13	Inmate	BMF
Curlen, James J.	WM	22	Lodger	NWS
Daidy, William A.	WM	17	Lodger	NWS
Daily, Fredrick	WM	18	Inmate	TMP

Daily, James P.	WM	19	Lodger	NWS
Daly, Margaret	WF	42	Servant	HBH
Danage, Crystal	WF	18	Lodger	EHG
Daniel, Clara	WF	17	Lodger	EHG
Danna, Salvator	WM	18	Inmate	TMP
Dauns, Mary	WF	20	Lodger	EHG
Davidson, Charles	WM	17	Inmate	TMP
DeLong, Victor	WM	18	Inmate	BMF
DeMair, Anthony	WM	17	Lodger	HBH
DeMars, Archie P.	WM	19	Inmate	BMF
DePalmer, Joseph	WM	16	Inmate	BMF
Devoe, Mabel	WF	18	Lodger	EHG
Dickenson, Gertrude	WF	18	Lodger	EHG
Dinde, Henry	WM	19	Lodger	44th
Distler, Alexander	WM	18	Lodger	44th
Doessler, George	WM	16	Lodger	HBH
Donin, Samuel	WM	13	Inmate	BMF
Donnelly, Alice	WF	52	Servant	HBH
Donovan, Leonora	WF	42	Servant	HBH
Dreslin, John	WM	3m	Inmate	ESW
Dreslin, Mary	WF	25	Inmate	ESW
Duffy, Edward	WM	15	Lodger	HBH
Duffy, Walter	WM	17	Lodger	HBH
Duncan, Raymond	WM	16	Lodger	35th
Dundge, Florence	WF	14	Lodger	EHG
Durra, Charles L.	WM	15	Inmate	TMP
Eagan, Matthew	WM	19	Lodger	NWS
Edmoston, William G.	WM	19	Lodger	44th
Ehrling, John	WM	17	Inmate	TMP
Eichler, Frank	WM	18	Lodger	HBH
Einstein, John	WM	17	Inmate	TMP
Eisner, William	WM	17	Inmate	TMP
Elinendorf, Edna	WF	14	Lodger	EHG
Engle, Jan	WM	16	Inmate	TMP
Enright, John	WM	17	Lodger	44th
Enright, Walter	WM	23	Porter	TMP
Enright, William	WM	16	Lodger	44th
Esk, Hugo	WM	18	Lodger	HBH
Ettinger, Morris	WM	18	Lodger	44th
Faber, Michael	WM	16	Inmate	TMP
Falern, Alfred	WM	16	Lodger	35th

Falvey, Howard	WM	10	Inmate	BMF
Farrall, Hugh J.	WM	19	Lodger	NWS
Farrar, Elizabeth	WF	55	Lodger	EHG
Farrell, William	WM	18	Lodger	35th
Farrschienge, Nellie	WF	17	Lodger	EHG
Fauer, Lizzie	WF	30	Lodger	EHG
Federman, Joseph	WM	17	Lodger	35th
Feicer, David	WM	18	Inmate	TMP
Ferber, Julius	WM	17	Inmate	TMP
Fernandez, Ladislow	WM	16	Inmate	BMF
Ferrello, Anthony W.	WM	20	Lodger	NWS
Finlay, Thomas	WM	17	Lodger	HBH
Fisher, Albert B.	WM	3	Son	BMF
Fisher, Charles P.	WM	39	Superintendant	BMF
Fisher, Charles	WM	17	Lodger	44th
Fisher, Harry	WM	16	Lodger	HBH
Fisher, James J.	WM	26	Lodger	NWS
Fisher, Joseph	WM	18	Inmate	TMP
Fisher, Marion B.	WF	32	Matron	BMF
Fitzgerald, Thos. J.	WM	16	Lodger	NWS
Flanagan, Ch. J.	WM	20	Lodger	NWS
Fleming, John	WM	18	Inmate	BMF
Fletcher, John	WM	18	Inmate	TMP
Fowler, George	WM	18	Lodger	35th
Fox, Max	WM	16	Lodger	44th
Francis, Ruth	WF	18	Lodger	EHG
Frannie, Thomas	WM	17	Inmate	BMF
Fuller, Carrie	WF	14	Lodger	EHG
Furman, Morris	WM	16	Inmate	TMP
Gallagher, John V.	WM	18	Lodger	NWS
Gannon, Edward F.	WM	18	Lodger	44th
Gartland, John Joseph	WM	18	Lodger	44th
Gartland, May	WF	10	Lodger	EHG
Gaugh, Ella	WF	21	Servant	BMF
Gaugh, Geroge	WM	31	Farm Laborer	BMF
Gedra, George	WM	27	Workman	HBH
Gellen, James	WM	17	Lodger	NWS
Gensberg, Michael	WM	18	Lodger	HBH
Gersen, Eddie	WM	18	Inmate	TMP
Gifford, John	WM	19	Lodger	44th
Gilland, Mary	WF	50	-	BMF

Gleason, James	WM	17	Lodger	HBH
Goldberg, Alexander	WM	17	Lodger	HBH
Goldberg, Herman	WM	16	Inmate	TMP
Goldfarb, Charles	WM	16	Lodger	44th
Goodwin, Arthur	WM	17	Lodger	44th
Gould, John	WM	45	Hired Man	BMF
Grand, Joseph	WM	17	Inmate	BMF
Grantzan, Margaret	WF	46	Lodger	EHG
Gray, Stozier	WM	19	Lodger	35th
Grecco, George J.	WM	19	Lodger	NWS
Gunn, Elizabeth	WF	24	Teacher	BMF
Gupfin, Frank J.	WM	19	Lodger	NWS
Gurisberg, Samuel	WM	17	Lodger	HBH
Hall, Narina	WF	14	Lodger	EHG
Halsey, Eugene	WM	27	Lodger	HBH
Hanan, Maud	WF	11	Lodger	EHG
Hannon, Thomas	WM	17	Lodger	HBH
Harriet, Chas. L.	WM	16	Lodger	NWS
Harrison, Nicholas	WM	17	Lodger	HBH
Hart, Joseph	WM	14	Lodger	44th
Hartley, Catherine	WF	17	Lodger	EHG
Hartman, William	WM	16	Lodger	HBH
Hatner, Max	WM	13	Inmate	BMF
Hawkins, Clarence	WM	6	Inmate	BMF
Hayes, Thomas	WM	16	Lodger	44th
Heffernan, Mary	WF	30	Caretaker	ESW
Heffernan, Paul	WM	5	Son	ESW
Heig, Andrew F.	WM	20	Son	NWS
Heig, Anna W.	WF	16	Daughter	NWS
Heig, Augusta M.	WF	48	Wife	NWS
Heig, Margaret A.	WF	18	Daughter	NWS
Heig, Oscar J.	WM	21	Son	NWS
Heig, Rudolph	WM	46	Head	NWS
Hein, Charles	WM	13	Lodger	HBH
Hein, George	WM	14	Lodger	HBH
Helirn, John J.	WM	17	Lodger	NWS
Hennefrund, Helen	WF	6mo.	Daughter	35th
Hennefrund, Henry	WM	27	Head	35th
Hennefrund, Willa	WF	20	Wife	35th
Herbert, Thomas	WM	17	Lodger	35th
Herniance, Earl	WM	10	Inmate	BMF

Herrara, Peter A.	WM	19	Lodger	NWS
Hertel, Edward	WM	16	Lodger	HBH
Hess, George	WM	15	Inmate	BMF
Higgins, Anthony	WM	18	Inmate	BMF
Hill, Anna Laura	WF	31	Visiting Agent	44th
Hill, William	WM	40	Painter	44th
Hirsch, Adolph	WM	17	Inmate	TMP
Hirsch, Morris	WM	16	Lodger	44th
Hoack, Gabriel T.	WM	17	Lodger	NWS
Hodson, Harry	WM	14	Inmate	BMF
Hoffman, Arthur	WM	19	Lodger	44th
Hohn, Ralph W.	WM	16	Lodger	NWS
Holarz, Margaret	WF	25	Servant	HBH
Holmes, Felix R.	WM	24	Lodger	NWS
Hoot, James	WM	17	Lodger	HBH
Hopke, Clarence	WM	17	Lodger	HBH
Hopkins, Joseph	WM	17	Lodger	44th
Howard, John	WM	11	Inmate	BMF
Hubert, Robert	WM	17	Lodger	44th
Hunt, Roy S.	WM	19	Lodger	NWS
Hussey, James	WM	18	Lodger	44th
Hyde, Katherine	WF	30	Teacher	BMF
Irocvy, George	WM	18	Lodger	HBH
Jack, William	WM	15	Lodger	HBH
Jacobs, Nathan	WM	18	Inmate	BMF
Jacobson, Jacob	WM	18	Lodger	35th
Jeane, Bella	WF	16	Lodger	EHG
Jewell, Ethel May	WF	20	Sister-in-Law	44th
Johnson, Anna	WF	29	Lodger	EHG
Johnson, John P.	WM	36	Engineer	35th
Johnson, Peter	WM	18	Lodger	HBH
Jones, Albert	WM	18	Lodger	HBH
Jones, Willard E.	WM	17	Lodger	NWS
Kaafnan, Henry H.	WM	17	Lodger	NWS
Kabela, Rudolph	WM	16	Inmate	BMF
Katz, Harry	WM	18	Lodger	NWS
Katz, Herman	WM	17	Inmate	TMP
Keane, Thomas	WM	20	Inmate	BMF
Kelley, Charles	WM	6	Inmate	BMF
Kelly, Anna J.	WF	22	Waitress	TMP
Kelly, Clara	WF	47	Matron	BMF

Kelly, James G.	WM	24	Lodger	NWS
Kelly, John H.	WM	16	Lodger	NWS
Kelly, John	WM	15	Lodger	44th
Kelly, John	WM	18	Inmate	BMF
Kelly, Peter	WM	18	Lodger	44th
Kelly, Thomas H.	WM	19	Lodger	NWS
Kenny, Albert	WM	17	Lodger	HBH
Keough, David	WM	15	Lodger	44th
Keugon, Abel	WM	63	Head	HBH
Keugon, Harry R.	WM	22	Son	HBH
Keugon, Sarah	WF	61	Wife	HBH
Klausner, Samuel	WM	18	Inmate	TMP
Klein, Edward	WM	16	Lodger	35th
Klein, Edward	WM	17	Inmate	TMP
Klein, Sam	WM	17	Inmate	TMP
Klug, Irving	WM	19	Lodger	44th
Knapp, Stanley	WM	17	Lodger	HBH
Krasel, Bernard	WM	17	Lodger	HBH
Krieger, Sam J.	WM	17	Lodger	NWS
Kupperman, Frank	WM	17	Inmate	TMP
Kutten, Harry J.	WM	17	Lodger	NWS
Lachman, Bernard H.	WM	13	Lodger	NWS
Lambert, George	WM	17	Inmate	BMF
Lanagan, John	WM	18	Lodger	44th
Langsen, William	WM	18	Lodger	44th
Leahy, John L	WM	17	Lodger	NWS
Leary, Chas. T.	WM	20	Lodger	NWS
Leary, John	WM	16	Lodger	HBH
Lehman, Louis	WM	17	Inmate	TMP
Leiberman, Harry S.	WM	16	Lodger	NWS
Leighton, Wm. M.	WM	16	Lodger	NWS
Lenahan, James	WM	17	Lodger	NWS
Lenahan, Patrick	WM	16	Inmate	BMF
Lenchner, Harry	WM	19	Inmate	BMF
Lennon, John J.	WM	17	Lodger	NWS
Leonard, Joseph D.	WM	23	Lodger	NWS
Lessinge, Morris	WM	18	Lodger	HBH
Levine, David	WM	17	Lodger	44th
Levine, Samuel	WM	16	Lodger	HBH
Levine, Thomas	WM	14	Inmate	BMF
Lewis, Harry	WM	17	Lodger	NWS

Lewis, Harry	WM	18	Lodger	NWS
Ley, Abram	WM	17	Lodger	35th
Lichtinar, Harry	WM	18	Lodger	HBH
Lighter, Louis	WM	17	Inmate	TMP
Lindauer, Fred	WM	17	Inmate	TMP
Logan, James	WM	16	Lodger	35th
London, Garfield T.	WM	16	Lodger	NWS
Lovell, Frederick H.	WM	49	-	HBH
Luger, Fred	WM	17	Lodger	HBH
Luther, Carl	WM	7	Inmate	BMF
Magiel, Arthur	WM	17	Lodger	NWS
Magniel, John J.	WM	16	Lodger	NWS
Maher, Robert	WM	16	Lodger	HBH
Maloy, Denis	WM	18	Lodger	44th
Mara, Frank	WM	15	Lodger	44th
Mara, John P.	WM	17	Lodger	44th
Marcus, Louis	WM	14	Inmate	TMP
Mariano, Josephine	WF	21	Lodger	EHG
Martin, John	WM	17	Inmate	BMF
Mason, Joseph	WM	17	Lodger	35th
McAlpin, Chester	WM	13	Inmate	BMF
McAvoy, James	WM	18	Lodger	NWS
McCabe, James J.	WM	26	Lodger	NWS
McCarthy, Mary J.	WF	37	Cook	TMP
McCorley, Leslie	WM	14	Lodger	HBH
McCormick, Joseph	WM	16	Lodger	HBH
McDonald, Agnes	WF	38	Lodger	EHG
McDonald, Bernard	WM	15	Lodger	44th
McEehenny, William	WM	16	Lodger	35th
McGowan, Edward	WM	18	Lodger	35th
McGowan, James E.	WM	17	Inmate	BMF
McKean, Edgar R.	WM	19	Son	TMP
McKean, Gertrud	WF	40	Wife	TMP
McKean, Jerom H.	WM	22	Son	TMP
McKean, Walter B.	WM	16	Son	TMP
McKean, William L.	WM	21	Son	TMP
McKean, William L.	WM	45	Superintendant	TMP
McKenzie, Frederick	WM	14	Inmate	BMF
McKibben, Hannah	WF	66	Asst. Matron	BMF
McKinna, Joseph J.	WM	19	Lodger	NWS
McMahon, John	WM	19	Lodger	NWS

Mc[illegible], Catherine	WF	23	Servant	BMF
Mednitsky, Abe	WM	17	Inmate	TMP
Meenan, John	WM	35	Porter	TMP
Metclay, Stella	WF	16	Lodger	EHG
Meyer, Gustave	WM	19	Lodger	44th
Middern, Eder S.	WM	27	Lodger	NWS
Miller, Ernest	WM	17	Lodger	35th
Miller, Jacob	WM	16	Inmate	TMP
Miller, Samuel	WM	17	Lodger	NWS
Millerstean, Louis	WM	18	Lodger	HBH
Millerstein, George	WM	18	Lodger	NWS
Minjiorn, Anthony	WM	17	Lodger	NWS
Minkel, Frank	WM	17	Lodger	HBH
Mintor, William	WM	18	Inmate	TMP
Monetti, Herbert	WM	20	Inmate	BMF
Monslopsky, Harry	WM	18	Lodger	HBH
Moore, Chas. E.	WM	18	Lodger	NWS
Moore, Wesley J.	WM	16	Lodger	NWS
Moran, Edward	WM	18	Lodger	35th
Moravec, Frank	WM	18	Inmate	BMF
Morino, John	WM	19	Lodger	NWS
Mortenson, Andrew	WM	33	Watchman	35th
Moses, Abraham	WM	18	Lodger	HBH
Mosher, Fred	WM	17	Lodger	44th
Mueller, James J.	WM	19	Lodger	NWS
Mulcahey, Roger I.	WM	16	Lodger	NWS
Mullen, Frank	WM	14	Lodger	HBH
Murdock, Frank	WM	17	Inmate	TMP
Murphy, Frank	WM	16	Lodger	44th
Murphy, Thomas	WM	17	Lodger	35th
Murray, Edward F.	WM	18	Lodger	NWS
Murray, Edward	WM	17	Lodger	HBH
Naiman, William	WM	14	Lodger	44th
Nelson, Joseph	WM	16	Lodger	35th
Neras, Joseph	WM	19	Inmate	BMF
Neumann, Anna M.	WF	37	Servant	NWS
Newman, Abraham	WM	17	Lodger	44th
Nilhos, George	WM	16	Lodger	35th
Nirdale, Peter	WM	19	Lodger	44th
Nolan, Mary	WF	49	Nurse	44th
Oberlander, Loouis	WM	17	Lodger	44th

O'Brady, Patrick	WM	18	Inmate	BMF
O'Brien, James	WM	16	Lodger	35th
O'Brien, Jeremiah	WM	16	Lodger	35th
O'Connell, Michael L.	WM	20	Lodger	35th
O'Connor, Everett	WM	10	Inmate	BMF
O'Connor, George	WM	16	Inmate	BMF
O'Connor, Vernon	WM	13	Inmate	BMF
Oeejo, Margerita	WF	1, 9m	Daughter	ESW
Oeejo, Margerita	WF	24	Laundress	ESW
Oelters, Harry	WM	16	Lodger	HBH
O'Keefe, William E.	WM	17	Lodger	NWS
Olsen, Holger O.	WM	17	Lodger	NWS
O'Mara, John	WM	15	Lodger	HBH
O'Neil, John	WM	18	Lodger	35th
O'Neill, Arthur	WM	18	Lodger	HBH
O'Neill, Joseph	WM	16	Inmate	BMF
Osborn, John	WM	18	Lodger	HBH
Otto, Bertha	WF	34	Lodger	EHG
Page, Norman	BM	14	Lodger	35th
Palmer, George G.	WM	18	Lodger	44th
Parascond, Frank	WM	14	Lodger	44th
Parker, Elizabeth	WF	55	Superintendant	EHG
Parker, Ella	WF	51	Asst. Super.	EHG
Parlantz, Justina	WF	15	Lodger	EHG
Parry, David W.	WM	27	Hired Man	BMF
Patterson, Archibald	WM	56	Asst. Manager	35th
Pearson, Peter A.	WM	15	Lodger	NWS
Perry, Joseph	WM	20	Lodger	NWS
Peters, Harry	WM	18	Lodger	HBH
Petrioke, Sylvester	WM	19	Lodger	HBH
Phenney, Catherine	WF	48	Servant	HBH
Pinto, Frank	WM	16	Lodger	NWS
Piscerra, Frank	WM	17	Lodger	44th
Pliner, Sashie	WF	17	Lodger	EHG
Pratley, Frederick	WM	16	Inmate	BMF
Price, Gertrude	WF	17	Lodger	EHG
Purtell, James P.	WM	19	Lodger	44th
Pyne, Thomas	WM	18	Lodger	35th
Quinn, Frank J.	WM	16	Lodger	NWS
Quinn, Laurence	WM	16	Lodger	35th
Quinn, Thos.	WM	17	Lodger	44th

Quirk, George	WM	17	Lodger	HBH
Quirke, Elsie	WF	15	Lodger	EHG
Ralston, Violla	WF	20	Lodger	EHG
Ranger, Nicholas G.	WM	24	Lodger	44th
Redness, David	WM	18	Lodger	35th
Regan, Frank	WM	18	Inmate	BMF
Reinhardt, Harry	WM	16	Inmate	BMF
Remick, Otto	WM	13	Inmate	BMF
Resnick, William	WM	16	Lodger	NWS
Reynolds, Bertha	WF	22	Lodger	EHG
Rice, Edmund A.	WM	20	Lodger	NWS
Rice, Ella	WF	28	Cook	ESW
Richards, Lizzie	WF	21	Lodger	EHG
Ritch, Jean A.	WM	16	Lodger	NWS
Riter, Harry	WM	17	Lodger	HBH
Roberts, Roynyne	WM	16	Lodger	HBH
Robinson, Henry	WM	19	Inmate	BMF
Robinson, Louis	WM	17	Lodger	HBH
Ross, Angelo	WM	17	Lodger	35th
Roth, Emanuel	WM	18	Lodger	NWS
Rothman, Morris	WM	17	Inmate	BMF
Rottman, Max	WM	19	Lodger	44th
Rourne, Thomas	WM	18	Lodger	44th
Rowan, John J.	WM	19	Lodger	NWS
Rubin, Leann	WF	14	Lodger	EHG
Ryan, Elizabeth	WF	16	Lodger	EHG
Ryan, John	WM	17	Lodger	35th
Ryback, Albert	WM	19	Lodger	44th
Sadler, Cyril	WM	18	Inmate	TMP
Santos, Gesta	WM	16	Lodger	NWS
Schermerhorn, John	WM	16	Inmate	BMF
Schick, Charles	WM	18	Inmate	BMF
Schmidt, George	WM	18	Inmate	TMP
Schneider, Louis	WM	16	Inmate	BMF
Schultz, Fred	WM	17	Lodger	35th
Schwartz, Harry	WM	17	Inmate	TMP
Schwartz, Isidor	WM	17	Inmate	TMP
Schwartz, Louis	WM	17	Inmate	TMP
Seaman, Anna	WF	16	Lodger	EHG
Seamnel, Julia	WF	55	Lodger	EHG
Sebot, Richard	WM	18	Lodger	35th

Seever, Joseph	WM	16	Lodger	35th
Seligman, William	WM	17	Inmate	TMP
Sellick, Joseph	WM	18	Inmate	TMP
Shabert, Harry	WM	18	Lodger	NWS
Shapiev, Abraham	WM	18	Lodger	44th
Shaw, Max	WM	17	Lodger	HBH
Shefford, Robert	WM	18	Lodger	35th
Sibatti, Joseph	WM	17	Lodger	44th
Sifoesnian, Max	WM	17	Lodger	HBH
Sigal, Meyer	WM	17	Inmate	TMP
Silver, Louis	WM	18	Inmate	TMP
Simponi, Michael	WM	17	Lodger	35th
Simpson, Lanida	WF	15	Lodger	EHG
Skelly, Philip	WM	17	Lodger	44th
Slatter, Minnie	WF	12	Lodger	EHG
Smalling, Sarah	WF	16	Lodger	EHG
Smelt, Kate	WF	17	Lodger	EHG
Smith, Arthur	WM	17	Inmate	BMF
Smith, Fred	WM	17	Inmate	TMP
Smith, Harry	WM	19	Lodger	44th
Smith, James A.	WM	16	Lodger	44th
Smith, James	WM	16	Lodger	44th
Smith, John	WM	18	Lodger	44th
Smith, William J.	WM	19	Lodger	44th
Smithers, Helen	WF	17	Lodger	EHG
Speller, Irving	WM	16	Lodger	35th
Spencer, Louis	WM	17	Inmate	TMP
Spier, Lotto	WF	17	Lodger	EHG
Spooner, Eastman	WM	10	Inmate	BMF
Stafilneski, Paul	WM	16	Inmate	TMP
Stanford, Ernest	BM	19	Inmate	BMF
Stanley, John	WM	17	Lodger	35th
Starkney, Walter	WM	16	Lodger	35th
Stasring, Frank	WM	17	Lodger	35th
Stein, Chas.	WM	16	Lodger	NWS
Stein, Jacob	WM	17	Lodger	HBH
Stein, Samuel	WM	18	Lodger	HBH
Steinberg, John	WM	14	Lodger	44th
Steiner, Julius	WM	17	Inmate	TMP
Stern, Eugene	WM	19	Lodger	35th
Stieglitz, Solomon	WM	18	Inmate	TMP

Stockey, William	WM	17	Lodger	44th
Stone, Chas. J.	WM	14	Lodger	NWS
Strobach, Paul J.	WM	17	Lodger	44th
Strohfeld, Benjamin	WM	16	Lodger	35th
Suden, Morris	WM	17	Lodger	NWS
Sugarman, William	WM	18	Inmate	TMP
Sullivan, James H.	WM	17	Lodger	NWS
Taylor, Thomas	WM	17	Lodger	35th
Thatcher, Everett	WM	15	Lodger	HBH
Thompson, Mary	WF	37	Lodger	EHG
Thorpe, Manley	WM	21	Janitor	44th
Tobias, Morris	WM	16	Lodger	HBH
Tretuler, Isidor	WM	17	Inmate	TMP
Trochart, Jacob	WM	18	Inmate	TMP
Tronchman, Jacob	WM	17	Inmate	TMP
Tucker, Howard	WM	11	Inmate	BMF
Uniors, Harry	WM	17	Lodger	35th
VanBuskirk, Carrrie	WF	24	Servant	BMF
Vanderbeck, George	WM	17	Lodger	44th
Vanderbeck, William	WM	15	Lodger	44th
VanDyke, Mary	WF	41	Wife	BMF
VanDyke, Ruth	WF	9	Daughter	BMF
VanDyke, William	WM	46	Farm Laborer	BMF
Vaughan, Thomas	BM	16	Lodger	35th
Victor, William	WM	18	Lodger	44th
Wagner, John P.	WM	21	Lodger	NWS
Walker, William	WM	16	Lodger	HBH
Walsh, Bartley	WM	17	Lodger	44th
Walsh, William	WM	17	Lodger	35th
Waters, James	WM	16	Lodger	HBH
Waters, Stephen	WM	18	Lodger	HBH
Weiner, Samuel	WM	17	Lodger	NWS
Weislurd, Samuel	WM	17	Inmate	TMP
Weisman, William	WM	20	Lodger	35th
Weiss, Morris	WM	17	Lodger	HBH
Welsh, Frank	WM	13	Lodger	44th
Whalen, John	WM	16	Lodger	44th
White, Regina	WF	16	Lodger	EHG
White, Samuel	WM	18	Lodger	44th
Whitley, Celia	WF	6	Inmate	ESW
Whitley, Pauline	WF	30	Inmate	ESW

Williams, Harry	BM	17	Lodger	35th
Williamson, Edward	WM	17	Inmate	BMF
Willis, Edward J.	WM	18	Lodger	44th
Willis, Richard	WM	17	Lodger	44th
Wilson, John	WM	16	Lodger	44th
Wilson, Samuel	BM	18	Inmate	TMP
Wimmar, Charles	WM	17	Lodger	44th
Winnans, Edna	WF	17	Lodger	EHG
Wolfe, George	WM	17	Inmate	BMF
Wolfe, Joseph	WM	16	Lodger	35th
Wood, Lillian B.	WF	37	Matron	44th
Wood, Mildred Jewell	WF	14m	Daughter	44th
Wood, William	WM	36	Superintendant	44th
Woods, John	WM	20	Inmate	BMF
Zevin, Solomon	WM	17	Inmate	BMF
Ziegler, John	WM	18	Inmate	TMP
Zind, Hilda	WF	25	Servant	NWS
Zoakee, Benjamin	WM	17	Lodger	HBH

1915

Guide to Column Headings

in the

1915 New York State Enumeration

Name Name of each person whose usual place of abode was in the institution on June 1, 1915. The census includes the name of every person living on June 1, 1915. Children born since June 1, 1915 were omitted. The surname is listed first, then the given name and middle initial.

R-G Race and gender. "White" is designated by "W", and "Black" by "B". Males are designated by "M" and "Females" by "F".

* Notes that the enumerator may have reported the name or gender incorrectly.

A Age at last birthday. Designated in years, unless otherwise noted with an "m" for "months" or "d" for "days". Generally, children who were less than one year old were described in terms of days, although some were described in terms of months.

Relation Relationship of each person to the institution.

LH Lodging House. The following lodging houses were included in this census:

35th: West Side Boys' Lodging House
225 West 35th Street
Assembly District 9, Election District 6

44th: Forty-Fourth Street Lodging House
247 East 44th Street
Assembly District 16, Election District 2

BMF: Brace Memorial Farm
Valhalla, Mount Pleasant,
Westchester County, Assembly District 3,
Enumeration District 6

EHG: Elizabeth Home for Girls
307 East 12th Street
Assembly District 10, Election District 19

ESW: Emergency Shelter for
Mothers with Children
307 East 12th Street
Assembly District 10, Election District 19

GHH: Goodhue Home
Prospect Avenue, New Brighten,
Richmond County
Assembly District 1, Election District 6

HBH: Harlem Boys' Hotel
136 East 127 Street
Assembly District 30, Election District 20

NWS: Newsboys' Lodging House
14 New Chambers Street
Assembly District 2, Election District 4

Note Refer to the orginal census for the nativity, citizenship, and occupation of residents.

Name	R-G	A	Relation	LH
Abrams, Herman	WM	19	Lodger	35th
Adams, Matthew	WM	40	Superintendant	GHH
Agerion, Tony	WM	23	Lodger	BMF
Andrew, Martin	WM	18	Lodger	HBH
Appleton, Robert	WM	17	Roomer	44th
Ariza, Generosia	WF	40	Boarder	EHG
Armstrong, Richard	WM	18	Lodger	HBH
Baker, Bertha S.	WF	42	Lodger	HBH
Baker, Herman	WM	46	Lodger	HBH
Banks, Jos.	WM	18	-	NWS
Bard, Gus	WM	20	Lodger	HBH
Barnett, Walter	WM	19	Lodger	35th
Bartley, Henry	WM	18	Roomer	NWS
Basacke, Otto	WM	19	Lodger	HBH
Bates, August	WM	19	Lodger	BMF
Bauer, William	WM	31	Kitchen Man	44th
Belfort, Thomas	WM	19	Lodger	BMF
Bell, Maud	WF	26	Boarder	EHG
Belly, Laura	WF	44	Boarder	EHG
Benway, Clara	WF	16	Boarder	EHG
Berge, Henry	WM	19	Lodger	HBH
Berge, Margaret	WF	46	Lodger	HBH
Beyer, Bertha	WF	42	Laundress	EHG
Biando, Joseph	WM	18	Roomer	44th
Blitzer, Elsie	WF	29	Helper	ESW
Blitzer, Harry	WM	4	Son	ESW
Bluherman, Benj.	WM	19	Roomer	NWS
Bodner, Isadore	WM	16	Roomer	44th
Bornstein, Morris	WM	18	Roomer	NWS
Boyce, James	WM	17	Lodger	BMF
Bradley, Anna	WF	19	Boarder	EHG
Brannworth, Louise	WF	22	Boarder	EHG
Bravo, Farribel	WM	17	Lodger	HBH
Breslin, Anna	WF	22	Boarder	EHG
Bresnahan, John	WM	18	Roomer	44th
Brooks, John J.	WM	17	Lodger	BMF
Brown, Jessie	WF	16	Boarder	EHG
Brown, John J.	WM	20	Lodger	35th
Browne, Harry U.	WM	20	Roomer	NWS

Buccheister, Joseph	WM 44	Gardiner	GHH
Budcher, William R.	WM 22	Ass't. Super.	35th
Burke, Edward	WM 18	Lodger	35th
Burke, John	WM 26	Janitor	44th
Burton, Harold	BM 17	Lodger	HBH
Butcher, May E.	WF 30	Mother	NWS
Butcher, Ruth	WF 2	Daughter	NWS
Butcher, Wm. L.	WM 7	Son	NWS
Butcher, Wm. L.	WM 30	Superintendant	NWS
Byrnes, Thomas	WM 20	Roomer	44th
Cameron, Robert E.	WM 18	Lodger	HBH
Cappazolo, Jennie	WF 20	Boarder	EHG
Carrol, James	WM 17	Lodger	BMF
Carroll, Frank J.	WM 17	Lodger	HBH
Cary, Phillip	WM 19	Roomer	44th
Casagrande, August	WM 15	Lodger	BMF
Casey, William J.	WM 19	Lodger	BMF
Cervillo, Joseph	WM 14	Lodger	BMF
Chester, George	WM 18	Lodger	BMF
Christie, Charles	WM 19	Lodger	HBH
Clarke, Lloyd	WM 15	-	NWS
Cline, Joseph	WM 19	Roomer	44th
Clint, Joseph	WM 19	Lodger	HBH
Coholan, Anna	WF 23	Helper	EHG
Coholan, Archibald	WM 6m	-	EHG
Colby, Adele	WF 29	Daughter-In-Law	ESW
Colby, George N.	WM 37	Son	ESW
Colby, Julia G.	WF 60	Superintendant	EHG
Cole, Fredrick	BM 16	Lodger	BMF
Colgan, John	WM 19	Lodger	35th
Collins, Mary	WF 22	Boarder	EHG
Conroy, John	WM 20	Roomer	NWS
Coons, Egbert	WM 18	Roomer	44th
Covino, Sam'l.	WM 18	Roomer	NWS
Coyle, Owen	WM 18	Roomer	44th
Crawford, Julien	WM 18	Roomer	44th
Crieg, Alfred	WM 19	Roomer	44th
Crosby, Arthur	WM 19	Lodger	BMF
Crotty, Timothy	WM 18	Lodger	BMF
Crozier, John P.	WM 18	-	NWS
Daley, Arthur J.	WM 17	Roomer	NWS

Daley, Jos. Jr.	WM	18	Roomer	NWS
Davis, Harry	WM	6	Lodger	BMF
Deitchman, Katherine	WF	19	Lodger	BMF
Deitchman, Mathew	WM	3d	Lodger	BMF
Deitchman, Samuel	WM	24	Lodger	BMF
Delabar, Dominic	WM	19	Lodger	HBH
Dewey, Harry	WM	16	Lodger	BMF
DiFretals, Oliver	WM	18	Lodger	HBH
Dimond, Fanny	WF	16	Boarder	EHG
Dolan, Jerry	WM	9	Lodger	BMF
Dolan, Sadie	WF	40	Cook	44th
Donino, Joseph	WM	18	Lodger	HBH
Dorsey, John	WM	18	-	NWS
Douglas, Herbert	WM	18	Lodger	HBH
Douglass, Grace	WF	22	Boarder	EHG
Drino, John	WM	18	Lodger	HBH
Drummond, Peter	WM	17	Lodger	BMF
Dugan, Edward	WM	17	Lodger	HBH
Dunidas, Susan	WF	39	Lodger	BMF
Dutt, Bejouls K.	WM	21	Roomer	NWS
Dwyer, John	WM	19	Lodger	BMF
Eagan, Mich'l.	WM	18	Roomer	NWS
Eagles, Geo. H.	WM	22	Roomer	NWS
Eck, Hugo	WM	25	Lodger	BMF
Edmondson, William	WM	17	Roomer	44th
Edwards, Jack	WM	17	Roomer	44th
Ellsworth, Virginia	WF	20	Boarder	EHG
Emmerson, Alfred	WM	72	Lodger	BMF
Engel, Joseph	WM	15	Lodger	35th
Englander, Herman	WM	19	Lodger	HBH
English, Arthur	WM	14	Lodger	BMF
Entwistle, William E.	WM	14	Lodger	35th
Farrar, Eliz. L.	WF	60	Matron	ESW
Farrell, Jos. B.	WM	19	Roomer	NWS
Farrell, Thomas J.	WM	17	Roomer	44th
Feldman, Benjamin	WM	18	Lodger	BMF
Fellner, Max	WM	19	Lodger	BMF
Fisher, Albert Bennet	WM	8	Son	HBH
Fisher, Charles P.	WM	45	Superintendant	HBH
Fisher, Marion	WF	36	Wife	HBH
Fisher, William A.	WM	17	Lodger	BMF

Fitzgerald, Thomas	WM	19	-	NWS
Flynn, William	WM	17	Roomer	44th
Fogarty, William	WM	20	Lodger	HBH
Force, Charles	WM	18	Lodger	BMF
Ford, John	WM	18	Lodger	BMF
Forrest, Lyonel	WM	19	Roomer	44th
Fox, Harry	WM	18	Lodger	35th
Frankel, Aaron	WM	18	Lodger	35th
Frealease, William H.	WM	19	Lodger	35th
Gallire, Wanke	WM	16	Lodger	35th
Ganout, William	WM	45	Ass't. Superintendant	HBH
Garino, John	WM	18	Roomer	NWS
Garson, Wm. J.	WM	19	Roomer	NWS
Gass, Charles	WM	16	Lodger	HBH
Gatily, Thomas	WM	15	Lodger	HBH
Gavin, Laurence	WM	18	Lodger	35th
Geldea, D.H.	WM	49	Lodger	35th
Gensler, Ellis	WM	20	Roomer	NWS
Gentile, Giovanie	WM	18	Lodger	35th
Gillen, Jos.	WM	18	Roomer	NWS
Glynn, Edward	WM	18	Lodger	BMF
Gold, John	WM	50	Lodger	BMF
Goldbaum, George	WM	17	Roomer	44th
Goldberg, Benj.	WM	18	Roomer	NWS
Gordon, Harry	WM	18	Lodger	BMF
Grantz, Minnie M.	WF	39	Assistant	EHG
Graywold, William	WM	16	Lodger	HBH
Green, Michael	WM	17	Lodger	BMF
Greend, Andrew	WM	19	Lodger	HBH
Greene, Walter	WM	18	Roomer	NWS
Gregor, John	WM	19	Brother	NWS
Gregor, Michael	WM	20	Brother	NWS
Griffen, Daniel	WM	18	Roomer	44th
Gross, Frieda	WF	19	Boarder	EHG
Grover, Nathan	WM	18	Roomer	44th
Hadd, Raymond	WM	20	Roomer	NWS
Hagan, William	WM	19	Roomer	44th
Halifax, Lucy	WF	22	Boarder	EHG
Hall, Raymond	WM	9	Lodger	HBH
Hanson, Paul	WM	18	Lodger	HBH
Harrigan, Agnes	WF	25	Waitress	EHG

Hart, Louis	WM	18	Lodger	HBH
Hawkins, Rob't. J.	WM	18	Lodger	35th
Hazelton, Wallace	WM	18	Roomer	44th
Heneghan, Thos.	WM	18	-	NWS
Hennefrund, Helen	WF	5	Daughter	44th
Hennefrund, Henry Jr.	WM	2	Son	44th
Hennefrund, Henry	WM	32	Superintendant	44th
Hennefrund, Willamenia	WF	26	Matron	44th
Hering, Peter	WM	15	Lodger	BMF
Higbee, Anna	WF	30	Teacher	GHH
Higgins, John	WM	18	Roomer	NWS
Hill, George	WM	17	Lodger	BMF
Hill, Tullis U.	WM	18	Roomer	NWS
Hobbs, Margaret	WF	45	Housekeeper	EHG
Hobehiss, William	WM	20	Lodger	HBH
Holloy, Rudolph	WM	14	Lodger	BMF
Hood, Katherine	WF	47	Lodger	BMF
Horn, Arthur	WM	19	Lodger	HBH
Horris, Harry	WM	18	Roomer	44th
Howard, Henry R.	WM	17	Lodger	35th
Hulands, Ida	WF	49	Lodger	BMF
Hunter, John	WM	19	Roomer	NWS
Hyde, Katherine	WF	unk.	Lodger	BMF
Jackson, Clara	WF	25	Boarder	EHG
Jackson, Clifford	BM	13	Lodger	35th
Jacobs, Iva	WF	29	Boarder	EHG
Jacobs, John	WM	18	Lodger	HBH
Jadot, Alphonse	WM	18	Lodger	35th
Johnson, Elizabeth	WF	24	Waitress	EHG
Johnson, George	WM	14	Lodger	BMF
Johnson, James E.	BM	50	Lodger	35th
Johnson, Theodore	WM	19	Lodger	BMF
Jones, Jenny	WF	28	Boarder	EHG
Jones, John C.	WM	26	Physical Director	35th
Jossel, Harry	WM	16	Lodger	35th
Kahns, Henry	WM	18	Lodger	HBH
Kaminsky, Solomon	WM	17	Lodger	BMF
Kane, George	WM	18	Roomer	44th
Keegan, Francis	WM	18	Lodger	35th
Kehler, Joseph	WM	18	Lodger	35th
Kelly, Edward	WM	17	Roomer	44th

Kelly, George	WM	18	Roomer	44th
Kelly, James	WM	20	Lodger	35th
Kempler, Frank	WM	21	Roomer	44th
Kempler, Joseph	WM	17	Roomer	44th
Kennedy, Thomas	WM	18	Lodger	35th
Kenzio, Roderick	WM	19	Lodger	BMF
Keogh, Anna	WF	19	Boarder	EHG
Kerns, Jennie	WF	30	Boarder	EHG
Kienzle, Ethel M.	WF	26	Lodger	BMF
Kienzle, Joseph	WM	27	Lodger	BMF
Kilkinny, Thomas P.	WM	19	Lodger	BMF
Kobbi, Annie	WF	31	Maid	EHG
Kobbi, Helen	WF	2	-	EHG
Krake, Jos.	WM	20	Roomer	NWS
Kranner, William	WM	19	Roomer	44th
Kreson, Dmitria	WM	29	Farm Hand	GHH
Kusbe, Henry	WM	14	-	NWS
Lackwood, Theodore	WM	16	Lodger	BMF
Landes, Herbert	BM	17	Lodger	BMF
Landis, Jos.	WM	16	-	NWS
Lane, Len.	WM	20	Adopted Son	GHH
Langer, Edward	WM	18	Lodger	HBH
Larsen, Charles	WM	17	Lodger	BMF
Leahey, David	WM	19	Roomer	44th
Leishman, Irene	WF	19	Boarder	EHG
Levey, Louis	WM	18	Roomer	44th
Lewis, Charles	WM	18	Lodger	HBH
Libby, Henry	WM	20	-	NWS
Linden, Louis	WM	25	Roomer	NWS
Loeb, Marie	WF	7m	-	ESW
Loeb, Mary	WF	33	Maid	ESW
Lutz, Francis	WM	11	Lodger	BMF
Mack, Ernst	WM	18	Roomer	44th
Mack, Louis	WM	18	Roomer	44th
Madden, Anna	WF	18	Boarder	EHG
Mais, Frank	WM	16	Lodger	35th
Mann, George	WM	14	Lodger	BMF
Marak, Mary	WF	23	Boarder	EHG
Martin, Harry	WM	19	Lodger	35th
Martin, William	WM	19	Lodger	35th
Mastusof, Abraham	WM	17	Lodger	BMF

May, Henry	WM	18	Roomer	NWS
Mayro, Joseph	WM	14	Lodger	35th
McCollich, Minnie	WF	24	Boarder	EHG
McCormick, Lawrence	WM	18	Roomer	NWS
McCroy, Jos.	WM	18	Roomer	NWS
McCullough, John	WM	18	Roomer	NWS
McDonald, Benjamin	WM	18	Roomer	44th
McDonald, John	WM	19	Lodger	HBH
McDonald, William	WM	19	Roomer	44th
McGann, William	WM	17	Lodger	HBH
McGrath, James	WM	18	Lodger	HBH
McGrath, Thos.	WM	17	-	NWS
McKenna, Chas.	WM	18	Lodger	35th
McKenzie, Jos.	WM	13	-	NWS
McKnight, James	WM	17	Roomer	44th
McStay, Kate	WF	28	Cook	GHH
Meiger, Alfred	WM	19	Roomer	44th
Melia, Sylvester	WM	18	Lodger	BMF
Mendes, Chas.	WM	20	Lodger	35th
Metalon, Alex	WM	18	Lodger	HBH
Meyer, Samuel	WM	14	Lodger	BMF
Michaels, Joseph	WM	17	Roomer	44th
Miley, Edward	WM	17	Lodger	HBH
Miller, Ernest	WM	19	Roomer	NWS
Miller, Henry	WM	18	Lodger	BMF
Miller, Samuel	WM	15	Lodger	BMF
Mills, Clarence	BM	19	Lodger	BMF
Moelkner, Ada	WF	17	Boarder	EHG
Moelkner, Bella	WF	22	Boarder	EHG
Moelkner, Laura	WF	18	Boarder	EHG
Moeller, Louis	WM	17	Lodger	35th
Mohn, Francis	WM	17	-	NWS
Monaghan, Phillip	WM	16	Roomer	44th
Mooney, Frank	WM	17	Roomer	44th
Moralis, Jenir	WM	19	Lodger	HBH
Moran, Edw.	WM	18	Roomer	NWS
Morris, Samuel	WM	17	Lodger	HBH
Moscowitz, Abe	WM	20	Lodger	HBH
Moskey, Samuel	WM	17	Lodger	35th
Mullane, Hugh	WM	17	Lodger	HBH
Mulligan, William	WM	19	Lodger	BMF

Murphy, Joseph	WM	16	Lodger	BMF
Murphy, Mary	WF	30	Teacher	GHH
Murphy, Robert	WM	19	Lodger	HBH
Myers, Wm.	WM	18	Lodger	35th
Nathan, Morris	WM	19	-	NWS
Nelson, Andrew	WM	18	Lodger	HBH
Nelson, Robert	WM	9	Lodger	BMF
Neuman, Harry	WM	19	Lodger	BMF
Newmar, Walter	WM	18	Lodger	HBH
Niles, John	WM	20	Roomer	NWS
Nolan, Mary	WF	51	Lodger	BMF
Norman, Max	WM	17	-	NWS
O'Connor, Margaret	WF	17	Boarder	EHG
O'Hara, William	WM	19	Lodger	HBH
Olden, Joseph	WM	17	Lodger	35th
Olsen, Harry	WM	19	Lodger	BMF
O'Mara, James	WM	17	Lodger	35th
O'Rourke, John	WM	17	Roomer	44th
O'Shaghnessy, Edward	WM	16	Lodger	35th
Parducci, Vito	WM	17	Roomer	44th
Perlman, Joseph	WM	20	Roomer	44th
Peterson, Caroline C.	WF	31	Lodger	BMF
Petlo, August	WM	18	Roomer	NWS
Pettit, John D.	WM	14	Lodger	BMF
Peyton, Walter	WM	16	Lodger	BMF
Pidgeon, Lester	WM	16	Lodger	BMF
Plimaka, Louis	WM	19	Roomer	NWS
Poland, Hattie	WF	43	-	NWS
Porter, Robert	WM	19	Lodger	HBH
Portugaise, Rose	WF	18	Boarder	EHG
Posthaner, Charles	WM	17	Lodger	BMF
Pound, Nathan	WM	11	Lodger	BMF
Pratt, Harry	WM	24	Lodger	35th
Pratt, Robert	WM	19	Lodger	HBH
Quartz, Francis C.	WM	21	Roomer	NWS
Radstosee, James	WM	18	Lodger	BMF
Ratner, Max	WM	16	Lodger	35th
Raun, Arnold	WM	15	-	NWS
Rayech, Leonard	WM	17	Roomer	44th
Reed, William	WM	18	Roomer	44th
Reifel, Estelle	WF	29	Boarder	EHG

Reilly, Edward	WM	17	Lodger	BMF
Rein, Lucille	WF	26	Boarder	EHG
Reynolds, Mary	WF	29	Boarder	EHG
Rikert, Dan'l.	WM	15	Roomer	NWS
Rodin, Hyman	WM	19	Roomer	NWS
Rosaler, Edward	WM	19	Lodger	35th
Ross, John A.	WM	19	Lodger	BMF
Russel, John	WM	16	Lodger	BMF
Ryan, John	WM	18	Roomer	NWS
Sabol, Edward	WM	18	Lodger	BMF
Saindoux, Marcus	WM	18	Lodger	35th
Salsfas, Issey	WM	17	-	NWS
Scanlon, John J.	WM	19	Lodger	BMF
Scanlon, Margaret	WF	38	Boarder	EHG
Schlager, Hedwig	WF	33	Boarder	EHG
Schmidt, Clara	WF	16	Boarder	EHG
Schroeder, Edward	WM	18	Lodger	HBH
Schultz, Edward	WM	16	Roomer	NWS
Schultz, Fred	WM	18	Lodger	35th
Schultz, George	WM	19	Lodger	35th
Schwam, Estelle	WF	21	Boarder	EHG
Seppa, Anna	WF	27	Cook	EHG
Shapiro, Morris	WM	16	-	NWS
Sherman, Hyman	WM	18	-	NWS
Silverra, George	WM	16	Lodger	HBH
Simpson, Edward	BM	15	Lodger	BMF
Slember, Gordon	WM	18	Lodger	HBH
Smith, Joe	WM	19	Lodger	35th
Smith, John	WM	17	Lodger	35th
Smith, Thos. E.	WM	18	Roomer	NWS
Smollen, Joseph	WM	18	Roomer	44th
Solz, Hyman	WM	16	Roomer	44th
Speciano, Augustus	WM	18	Lodger	BMF
Spence, John	WM	19	Lodger	35th
Spillman, Anna	WF	26	Boarder	EHG
Spring, Henry I.	WM	32	Roomer	NWS
Spry, Sadie	WF	23	Boarder	EHG
Stamper, Jeanette	WF	25	Boarder	EHG
Stanford, John	WM	17	Lodger	BMF
Stark, Jos.	WM	18	Roomer	NWS
Steinhaus, Sadie	WF	19	Boarder	EHG

Sternburg, Nathan	WM 18	Lodger	35th
Stewart, Wm. F.	WM 23	Roomer	NWS
Stroffin, Howard A.	WM 26	Superintendant	35th
Styer, Yetta	WF 20	Boarder	EHG
Sullivan, Michael	WM 19	Roomer	44th
Sundberg, Charles	WM 18	Lodger	HBH
Sweeny, Miles	WM 18	Lodger	HBH
Talbe, Walter H.	WM 15	-	NWS
Taylor, John	WM 17	Lodger	HBH
Thompson, Hazel	BF 17	Lodger	35th
Thornton, Frank	WM 21	Roomer	44th
Thorpe, Katherine	WF 26	Lodger	BMF
Tobrick, Sam'l.	WM 18	Roomer	NWS
Tompkins, Frank	WM 18	Lodger	HBH
Towers, Adeline	WF 22	Chambermaid	44th
Townsend, Chas.	WM 19	Lodger	35th
Tunmino, John D.	WM 18	Roomer	NWS
Tyczko, Stephen	WM 17	Lodger	BMF
Underhill, Ruth	BF 40	Lodger	35th
VanSchmidt, Charles	WM 18	Lodger	HBH
Vrousalous, Polyxene	WF 25	Boarder	EHG
Wagh, John R.	WM 17	Roomer	NWS
Wagner, Philip	WM 19	Roomer	44th
Walsh, Frank	WM 18	Roomer	44th
Walsh, Mamie	WF 24	Boarder	EHG
Walsh, Thomas Jr.	WM 19	-	NWS
Walsh, Thomas	WM 16	Lodger	BMF
Walter, Adolph	WM 18	Lodger	35th
Warren, Harry	WM 18	Lodger	HBH
Weatherbee, Mollie	WF 20	Boarder	EHG
Webber, Louise	WF 19	Boarder	EHG
Weiss, Isadore	WM 17	Roomer	44th
Welinski, Michael	WM 30	Farm Hand	GHH
Wenger, Robert	WM 18	Lodger	35th
Wesley, Harold B.	WM 19	Roomer	NWS
Whalen, Edw. J.	WM 18	Roomer	NWS
White, Albert	WM 17	Lodger	BMF
Whitman, John	WM 17	Roomer	44th
Wiener, Solomon	WM 13	Lodger	BMF
Williams, Mary	WF 25	Teacher	GHH
Williamson, John	WM 6	Lodger	BMF

Wilson, Chas.	WM	19	Roomer	NWS
Winans, Edna	WF	21	Maid	EHG
Wincoop, Allen	WM	18	Roomer	44th
Wolfe, Max	WM	19	Lodger	HBH
Wood, Lillian B.	WF	42	Wife	BMF
Wood, Mildred	WF	6	Daughter	BMF
Wood, William S.	WM	41	Superintendant	BMF
Wright, Edwin	WM	12	Son	BMF
Wright, Edwin	WM	52	Head	BMF
Wright, Hector	WM	14	Son	BMF

1920

Guide to Column Headings

in the

1920 Federal Enumeration

Name — Name of each person whose usual place of abode was in the institution on January 1, 1920. The census includes the name of every person living on January 1, 1920. Children born since January 1, 1920 were omitted. The surname is listed first, then the given name and middle initial.

R-G — Race and gender. White is designated by "W", and "Black" by "B". "Males" are designated by "M" and "Females" by "F".

***** — Notes that the enumerator may have reported the name or gender incorrectly.

A — Age at last birthday. Designated in years, unless otherwise noted with an "m" for "months".

Relation — Relationship of each person to the institution.

LH — Lodging House. The following lodging houses were included in this census:

35th: West Side Lodging House
225 West 35th Street
Enumeration District 294

BMF: Brace Memorial Farm
Valhalla, Mount Pleasant,
Westchester County
Enumeration District 73

EHG: Elizabeth Home for Girls
307 East 12th Street
Enumeration District 651

ESW: Emergency Shelter for
Women with Children
311 East 12th Street
Enumeration District 651

GHH: Goodhue Home
Prospect Avenue, New Brighton,
Richmond County
Enumeration District 1552

HBH: Harlem Boys' Hotel
136 East 127th Street
Enumeration District 1398

LEH: A. Louise Erlanger Home
442 West 23rd Street
Enumeration District 268

NWS: Newsboys' Lodging House
244 William Street
Enumeration District 53

Note — Refer to the orginal census for the nativity, language, citizenship, and education of each resident.

Name	R-G	A	Relation	LH
Adams, Bertha	WF	36	Boarder	EHG
Allen, Charles	WM	10	Inmate	BMF
Anderson, Maude	WF	32	Wife	HBH
Anderson, Olivia	WF	34	Boarder	EHG
Anderson, Raymond L.	WM	34	Superintendant	HBH
Arah, Minnie	WF	22	Boarder	EHG
Aurigemma, Eugenia	WF	9	Inmate	GHH
Austin, Harold	WM	10	Inmate	BMF
Bannister, Fred	WM	25	Boarder	NWS
Beck, Anna	WF	20	Boarder	EHG
Berman, Dora	WF	23	Boarder	EHG
Birch, Helen	WF	18	Boarder	EHG
Blose, William	WM	13	Inmate	BMF
Blukus, Michael	WM	42	Gardiner	GHH
Blum, Catherine	WF	53	Mother	35th
Blum, Ernest	WM	63	Father	35th
Blum, George	WM	34	Head	35th
Blum, Susan	WF	32	Wife	35th
Bovincino, Concetta	WF	8	Inmate	GHH
Bradford, Albert	BM	8	Inmate	BMF
Brush, William Frances	WM	8	Inmate	BMF
Buchheister, Joseph C.	WM	49	Gardiner	GHH
Burke, Josephine	WF	41	Boarder	EHG
Calamari, Frank	WM	19	Boarder	NWS
Caldwell, George D.	WM	51	Boarder	EHG
Cappell, Helen	WF	8	Inmate	GHH
Caracciolo, Brigida	WF	10	Inmate	GHH
Casey, John	WM	25	Boarder	NWS
Catalvotto, Charlie	WM	16	Boarder	NWS
Clate, Peter	WM	8	Inmate	BMF
Claus, Minnie	WF	?8	Boarder	EHG
Clirssee, Florence	WF	22	Boarder	EHG
Colby, Julia	WF	46	Superintendant	EHG
Compton, Emeline	WF	31	Boarder	EHG
Condia, Angelina	WF	7	Inmate	GHH
Cory, Alice	WF	19	Boarder	EHG
Cote, Joseph	WM	23	Boarder	NWS
Crabb, Charles	WM	10	Inmate	BMF
Craft, Jerry	WM	24	Boarder	NWS

Cramer, Veryl	WM	8	Inmate	BMF
Crimon, Dorothy	WF	19	Boarder	EHG
Dauria, Peter P.	WM	17	Boarder	NWS
Davis, Jack	WM	18	Boarder	NWS
DeLucca, Albert	WM	20	Boarder	NWS
Densa, Florence	WF	17	Daughter	LEH
Densa, Harriet	WF	51	Caretaker	LEH
DeSoto, Louise	WF	29	Boarder	EHG
Dorfnan, Rose	WF	23	Boarder	EHG
Eagan, Michael	WM	25	Lodger	NWS
Ech, Hugo	WM	30	Servant	BMF
Edwards, August	WM	12	Inmate	BMF
Elston, Elija	WM	48	Ass't. Super.	BMF
Elston, Flora	WF	48	Matron	BMF
Etheridg, Blanche	WF	29	Nurse	GHH
Farrel, Lawrence	WM	4	Son	ESW
Farrel, Rose	WF	24	Head	ESW
Fay, John	WM	7m	Son	ESW
Fay, Ma[illegible] F.	WF	22	Daughter	ESW
Fay, Tillie	WF	54	Head	ESW
Fein, Yetta	WF	9	Inmate	GHH
Finley, Howard	WM	17	Boarder	NWS
Fiorellino, Annie	WF	8	Inmate	GHH
Fitzgerald, May	WF	22	Boarder	EHG
Fitzpatrick, Veronica	WF	12	Inmate	GHH
Fleming, Annie	WF	9	Inmate	GHH
Forbes, Rosemary	WF	9	Inmate	GHH
Foster, Howard	WM	18	Inmate	BMF
French, Lucie	WF	44	Seamstress	LEH
Friscia, Antoinette	WF	8	Inmate	GHH
Gabidino, Joseph	WM	18	Boarder	NWS
Gardiner, Beatrice	WF	15	Boarder	GHH
Gardiner, Evelyn	WF	16	Boarder	GHH
Gardoska, John	WM	3	Boarder	GHH
Genaler, Ellis	WM	27	Boarder	NWS
Gludenis, Francis	WM	15	Boarder	NWS
Gold, Ida	WF	53	Wife	BMF
Gold, John	WM	55	Engineer	BMF
Goldstein, Abraham	WM	16	Boarder	NWS
Goodman, Blanche	WF	11	Inmate	GHH
Gorvaty, Millie	WF	19	Boarder	EHG

Granieri, Guiseppe	WM	20	Boarder	NWS
Greene, Rose	WF	24	Boarder	EHG
Hanley, Annie Bridget	WF	37	Servant	BMF
Hanley, George	WM	5	Son	BMF
Hanley, William	WM	6m	Son	BMF
Harissman, Anna	WF	43	Servant	BMF
Hawkes, Thomas	WM	28	Clerk	HBH
Hays, Anna May	WF	22	Boarder	EHG
Herman, Louise	WF	20	Boarder	EHG
Heym, Frerick John	WM	16m	Son	BMF
Heym, Harry Robert	WM	23	Farmer	BMF
Heym, Lucy E.	WF	20	Wife	BMF
Hill, Maurice	BM	17	Inmate	BMF
Hirsch, Edna	WF	12	Inmate	GHH
Horalambo, Faselilha	WF	24	Boarder	EHG
Howard, Mildred	WF	27	Boarder	EHG
Huestes, Edna	WF	18	Boarder	EHG
Hughes, Edward J.	WM	18	Boarder	NWS
Hzayler, David	WM	17	Boarder	NWS
Irna, Mary	WF	29	Boarder	EHG
Irwhurst, Adeline	WF	36	Boarder	EHG
Jeterlanyn, Theresa	WF	17	Boarder	EHG
Johnson, Andrew	WM	34	Head	GHH
Johnson, Christine	WF	24	Wife	GHH
Johnson, Donald	WM	5	Son	GHH
Johnson, Heather	WF	2	Daughter	GHH
Johnson, Joseph	WM	27	Boarder	NWS
Johnson, Mamie L.	WF	37	Wife	GHH
Johnson, William F.	WM	42	Head	GHH
Johnson, William G.	WM	10	Son	GHH
Jordan, Herbert	WM	18	Boarder	NWS
Julian, Sarah	WF	25	Boarder	EHG
Kansella, Lillian	WF	18	Boarder	EHG
Keeley, Thomas	WM	unk.	Lodger	HBH
Kelly, Edward	WM	16	Boarder	NWS
Kelly, John F.	WM	28	Boarder	NWS
Ketolon, Anthony	WM	4	Son	ESW
Ketolon, Helin	WF	35	Head	ESW
Knechta, George	WM	15	Boarder	NWS
Kowalski, Anthony	WM	21	Boarder	NWS
Kozlow, Michael	WM	20	Boarder	NWS

Krovich, Benjamin	WM	15	Inmate	BMF
LaDuca, Ottaviana	WF	7	Inmate	GHH
Lawrence, Andrew	BM	13	Inmate	BMF
Leahy, John	WM	21	Boarder	NWS
Lenihan, John	WM	17	Boarder	NWS
Lennon, John	WM	27	Boarder	NWS
Lenoff, Solomon	WM	24	Boarder	NWS
Levine, Minnie	WF	12	Inmate	GHH
Levitan, Celia	WF	5	Inmate	GHH
Levitan, Gertrude	WF	11	Inmate	GHH
Lewis, Hazel	WF	25	Teacher	GHH
Lima, Mary	WF	9	Inmate	GHH
Lima, Ottavia	WF	8	Inmate	GHH
Lloyd, Anna	WF	16	Boarder	EHG
Lobick, Samuel	WM	24	Engineer	HBH
Locsher, Caroline	WF	18	Cook	BMF
Lonard, Lena	WF	38	Servant	BMF
Lonard, Paul	WM	10	Son	BMF
Lorenzo, Rosie	WF	9	Inmate	GHH
Lucas, John	WM	18	Inmate	BMF
Lucas, May	WF	33	Head	EHG
Maas, William	WM	15	Boarder	NWS
MacDwyer, Effie	WF	23	Boarder	EHG
MacKeagan, Christine	WF	23	Boarder	EHG
Maxwell, Carrie	WF	40	Head	EHG
Maxwell, May	WF	6	Daughter	EHG
McAndrew, John	WM	27	Boarder	NWS
McAvoy, Thomas	WM	21	Boarder	NWS
Mechini, Sylvia	WF	8	Inmate	GHH
Morgan, Ella	WF	23	Boarder	EHG
Mostkich, Sallie	WF	20	Boarder	EHG
Muffa, Rose	WF	18	Boarder	EHG
Myerentina, Marcelina	WF	8	Inmate	GHH
Newman, Edith	WF	17	Boarder	EHG
O'Connor, Philip	WM	24	Clerk	HBH
Osmond, Florence	WF	10	Inmate	GHH
Paterno, Antonette	WF	7	Inmate	GHH
Pawloski, Thomas	WM	17	Boarder	NWS
Pearson, Leo.	WM	16	Boarder	NWS
Pessex, Simon	WM	17	Boarder	NWS
Peters, Irene	WF	13	Inmate	GHH

Peterson, Caroline	WF	35	Superintendant	LEH
Peterson, Mae	WF	26	Boarder	EHG
Philips, Ruben	WM	17	Lodger	35th
Pierce, George	WM	16	Boarder	NWS
Pietrowski, Daniel	WM	20	Boarder	NWS
Pietrowski, Felix	WM	15	Boarder	NWS
Pirpenbrick, Fred	WM	14	Inmate	BMF
Poole, Charles	WM	14	Boarder	NWS
Portworsitz, Ida	WF	6	Inmate	GHH
Post, Herbert	WM	6	Inmate	BMF
Pound, Nathan	WM	16	Inmate	BMF
Primavera, Sadie	WF	10	Inmate	GHH
Prousalona, Polyana	WF	24	Boarder	EHG
Pryon, Olive	WF	20	Boarder	EHG
Punsarna, Louise	WF	22	Boarder	EHG
Quimiz, Edward	WM	16	Boarder	NWS
Rajala, Ambrose	WM	15	Boarder	NWS
Regan, Katharine	WF	24	Boarder	EHG
Reinhardt, Ida	WF	60	Servant	BMF
Rice, Catharine	WF	22	Boarder	EHG
Ricordi, Margaret	WF	9	Inmate	GHH
Robertson, Arthur	WM	20	Boarder	NWS
Rodgers, Frank	WM	20	Boarder	NWS
Rosansky, Rose	WF	7	Inmate	GHH
Rosengreen, Eric	WM	21	Boarder	NWS
Rosenthal, Tussie	WF	7	Inmate	GHH
Rosenwitz, Anna	WF	25	Boarder	EHG
Roufosse, Ethel	WF	26	House Mother	GHH
Roufosse, Marie	WF	6	Boarder	GHH
Row, John	WM	14	Inmate	BMF
Rumpt, Elizabeth	WF	35	Boarder	EHG
Scanlin, Margaret	WF	38	Boarder	EHG
Schiam, Stella	WF	26	Boarder	EHG
Schimarich, Eva	WF	35	Boarder	EHG
Schipsky, Margaret	WF	20	Boarder	EHG
Schwalbe, Catherine	WF	9	Inmate	GHH
Schwartz, William	WM	20	Boarder	NWS
Sethman, Walter	WM	8	Inmate	BMF
Sevine, Samuel	WM	19	Inmate	BMF
Seymour, Arthur	WM	7	Inmate	BMF
Sidel, Anna	WF	17	Boarder	EHG

Siedel, Harris	WM	15	Inmate	BMF
Siventzal, Viola	WF	26	Boarder	EHG
Spellman, Kathrine	WF	18	Boarder	EHG
Sradway, Felix	BM	17	Inmate	BMF
Steinberg, Bertha	WF	10	Inmate	GHH
Stio, Rosina	WF	7	Inmate	GHH
Strauf, James	WM	15	Inmate	BMF
Sugo, Antonio	WM	12	Inmate	BMF
Thirstophig, Dorothy	WF	6m	Daughter	EHG
Thristophig, Minnie	WF	32	Head	EHG
Tracy, Austin	WM	14	Inmate	BMF
Traynor, Robert	WM	20	Boarder	NWS
Valansy, Elizabeth	WF	17	Boarder	EHG
VanHagen, Charles	WM	14	Inmate	BMF
Vause, Paul	WM	9	Inmate	BMF
VonBychet, Martha	WF	20	Boarder	EHG
Wagner, Anna W.	WF	48	Head	ESW
Wagner, Anna	WF	13m	Daughter	ESW
Wagner, Ericka	WF	22m	Boarder	GHH
Wagner, Joseph	WM	0m	Son	ESW
Wagner, Lucy	WF	31	Teacher	GHH
Warclan, A[illegible]	WF	19	Boarder	EHG
Weatke, Helen	WF	36	Cook	LEH
Wesley, Harold	WM	24	Boarder	NWS
Wicks, Emily	WF	14	Boarder	GHH
Wicks, Katherine	WF	39	Matron	GHH
Williams, Major	BM	12	Inmate	BMF
Wilt, Frances	WF	7m	Daughter	ESW
Wilt, Joseph	WM	5	Son	ESW
Wilt, Mary	WF	35	Head	ESW
Wittran, Sarah	WF	29	Boarder	EHG
Wood, Lillian	WF	47	Wife	BMF
Wood, Mildred	WF	16	Daughter	BMF
Wood, William	WM	46	Superintendant	BMF
Yensin, Frieda	WF	24	Head	EHG
Yensin, L[illegible]	WF	4m	Daughter	EHG
Ylucery, Veronica	WF	24	Boarder	EHG
Zarecka, Helen	WF	5m	Boarder	GHH
Zarecka, Kazmiera	WF	26	Servant	GHH
Zelt, B[illegible]	WF	3	Daughter	EHG
Zelt, Kathrine	WF	34	Matron	EHG

Zelt, Lillian	WF	15	Daughter	EHG
Zerota, Harry	WM	15	Boarder	NWS
Zobel, Elizabeth	WF	?	Boarder	EHG
Zury, Andrew	WM	19	Boarder	NWS

1925

Guide to Column Headings

in the

1925 New York State Enumeration

Name Name of each person whose usual place of abode was in the institution on June 1, 1925. The census includes the name of every person living on June 1, 1925. Children born since June 1, 1925 were omitted. The surname is listed first, then the given name and middle initial.

R-G Race and gender. "White" is designated by "W", and "Black" by "B". "Males" are designated by "M" and "Females" by "F".

* Notes that the enumerator may have reported the name or gender incorrectly.

A Age at last birthday. Designated in years, unless otherwise noted with an "m" for "months" or "d" for "days".

Relation Relationship of each adult to the institution. The relationship of each child to the institution was not included.

LH Lodging House. The following lodging houses were included in this census:

BMF: Brace Memorial Farm
Valhalla, Mount Pleasant,
Westchester County
Assembly District 3, Election District 7

EHG: Elizabeth Home for Girls
307 East 12th Street
Assembly District 8, Election District 22

ESW: Emergency Shelter for
Women with Children
311 East 12th Street
Assembly District 8, Election District 22

GHH: Goodhue Home
Prospect Avenue, New Brighton,
Richmond County
Assembly District 1, Election District 12

HBH: Harlem Boys' Hotel
136 East 127th Street
Assembly District 20, Election District 8

KBB: Kip's Bay Boys' Home
825 Second Avenue
Assembly District 12, Election District 36

MBM: Martha Home (at Brace Memorial Farm)
Valhalla, Mount Pleasant,
Westchester County
Assembly District 3, Election District 7

NWS: Newsboys' Lodging House
244 William Street
Assembly District 1, Election District 19

Note Refer to the original census for the nativity, citizenship, education, and occupation of residents.

Name	R-G	A	Relation	LH
Ahearn, Michael	WM	19	Roomer	KBB
Anderson, Charles	WM	5	-	BMF
Anderson, Raymond	WM	38	Superintendant	HBH
Anderson, Willis	WM	4	-	BMF
Andrews, Emma	WF	41	Employee	EHG
Barrett, Andrew	WM	4	-	BMF
Bashune, Atheins	WF	22	Boarder	EHG
Bashune, Emily	WF	20	Boarder	EHG
Bass, Aaron	WM	18	-	MBM
Beattie, Frank	WM	18	Roomer	KBB
Beauchaan, Albert	WM	20	Roomer	KBB
Berry, William	WM	65	Watchman	NWS
Bishop, Charles	WM	11	-	BMF
Blair, Stephen	WM	19	Roomer	KBB
Block, Sam	WM	17	Roomer	KBB
Boddion, Arthur	WM	19	Roomer	KBB
Boeds, James	WM	13	-	BMF
Bowen, Wilma	WF	15	Inmate	GHH
Brenkus, John	WM	17	Roomer	KBB
Britton, Graven	WM	9	-	BMF
Britton, Leslie	WM	8	-	BMF
Brown, James	BM	13	-	BMF
Brtoloth, George	WM	14	-	MBM
Buccheister, John	W-	60	Gardner	GHH
Bundy, Leslie	WM	9	-	BMF
Caldsi, Concepta	WF	31	Boarder	EHG
Canfield, Alice	W-	26	Teacher	GHH
Cardinal, Frank	WM	17	Roomer	KBB
Carney, Margaret	WF	32	Boarder	EHG
Carr, Thomas	WM	52	Roomer	HBH
Case, Hazel A.	W-	24	Supervisor	GHH
Cassidy, Joseph	WM	30	Secretary	NWS
Chadell, Max	WM	19	Roomer	KBB
Chadsy, Roy J.	WM	18	Roomer	KBB
Chadwick, Bessie	WF	26	Boarder	EHG
Chadwick, Emma	WF	25	Boarder	EHG
Chamberlain, Harold	W-	25	Staff	GHH
Charter, Armond	WM	18	Roomer	KBB
Closs, Sara	WF	9	Inmate	GHH

Clutterbuck, Joseph	WM	8	-	BMF
Colby, Julia G.	WF	72	Superintendant	EHG
Collone, Helen	WF	20	Boarder	EHG
Connell, William	WM	21	Boarder	NWS
Connelly, Bernard	WM	16	-	BMF
Connors, Richard	WM	63	Boarder	KBB
Conroy, James	WM	19	Roomer	KBB
Cooy, Nicholas	WM	17	Boarder	NWS
Copeland, Charles	WM	45	Engineer	HBH
Core, Helen	WF	29	Boarder	EHG
Crump, Harriett	WF	50	Seamstress	BMF
Dames, Catherine	WF	55	Employee	EHG
Danes, Dorothy	WF	16	Boarder	EHG
Danielson, Henry	WM	18	Roomer	KBB
Dartt, Fred	WM	18	Roomer	KBB
Davis, Elsie	WF	7	Inmate	GHH
Davis, Lester	WM	5	-	BMF
Davis, Louis	WM	10	-	BMF
Davis, Marie	WF	2	Inmate	GHH
Dean, Edward	WM	26	Roomer	KBB
Debella, Salvatore	WM	18	Roomer	KBB
Delbosso, John	WM	20	Roomer	KBB
Denbam, Charles	WM	15	-	BMF
Denney, Joseph	WM	11	-	MBM
Dessoir, Emma	WF	20	Boarder	EHG
Devine, Willa	WF	4	Inmate	GHH
Dickenson, George	WM	19	Roomer	KBB
Dignacca, Josie	WF	30	Boarder	EHG
Dinner, Abraham	WM	17	Roomer	KBB
Dinni, May	WF	31	Employee	EHG
Dinni, Willie	WM	2	-	EHG
Donathoone, Agnes	WF	22	Boarder	EHG
Dumouette, Roland	WM	19	-	BMF
Dutcher, William	WM	8	-	BMF
Dwyer, Helen	WF	20	Boarder	EHG
Dywcneyzk, Saudia	WF	22	Boarder	EHG
Earl, Harvey	WM	13	-	BMF
Edmondson, Wm.	WM	27	Roomer	KBB
Eisner, Louis	WM	23	Roomer	KBB
Ellsworth, Edgar	WM	5	-	BMF
English, Jack	WM	18	Roomer	KBB

Fairfield, Raymond	WM	10	-	BMF
Farrier, John	BM	33	Husband	KBB
Farrier, Lucy	BF	27	Wife	KBB
Fassiani, Vincent	WM	17	Roomer	KBB
Fay, James	WM	17	Roomer	KBB
Fay, Martin	WM	18	Roomer	KBB
Felton, Fred	WM	24	Chauffeur	BMF
Ferguson, Elise M.	WF	70	Matron	EHG
Ferguson, Joseph	BM	10	-	BMF
Ferrera, Anna	WF	13	Inmate	GHH
Fitzgerald, Mary	WF	17	Boarder	EHG
Fox, Harry	WM	12	-	MBM
French, Lucy T.	W-	25	Supervisor	GHH
Fuechtuanger, Ernest	WM	11	-	BMF
Garfield, Albert	WM	16	Roomer	KBB
Garrbants, Robert	WM	16	-	BMF
Gentile, Dan	WM	20	Roomer	KBB
Gerintho, Emanuel	WM	17	Boarder	NWS
Getzinger, Evelyne	WF	18	Boarder	EHG
Gilman, Max	WM	18	Roomer	KBB
Giodowsky, Frances	WF	18	Boarder	EHG
Gionoviah, Sofie	WF	22	Boarder	EHG
Glopenburgh, Mildred	WF	18	Boarder	EHG
Gobling, Fred	WM	65	Engineer	NWS
Golden, Howard	WM	13	-	BMF
Golis, Elizabeth	WF	18	Boarder	EHG
Golis, Marion	WF	21	Boarder	EHG
Gordon, Joseph	WM	42	Welfare Worker	NWS
Gowitz, Mildred	WF	23	Boarder	EHG
Grantz, Minnie M.	WF	49	Asst. Super.	EHG
Gross, Harry	WM	17	Roomer	KBB
Guarascio, Domenick	WM	18	Roomer	KBB
Guggenthal, James	WM	17	Boarder	NWS
Halvey, Joseph	WM	18	Roomer	KBB
Hanson, Walter	WM	19	Roomer	KBB
Harchell, Chas.	WM	18	Roomer	KBB
Harelamiltoi, Vaselike	WF	38	Boarder	EHG
Harmant, Wm. T.	WM	19	Roomer	KBB
Hartart, Patrick	WM	48	Farm Manager	BMF
Hawkes, Thomas	WM	33	Club Director	HBH
Hicks, Clarence	BM	13	-	BMF

Hill, Wilbur J.	WM	50	Welfare Worker	NWS
Huck, Arthur	WM	4	Child	KBB
Huck, Arthur	WM	33	Superintendant	KBB
Huck, Georgina	WF	9	Child	KBB
Huck, Georgina	WF	35	Wife	KBB
Huck, John	WM	2	Child	KBB
Hull, Minnie	WF	45	Employee	EHG
Hunter, Alfred	BM	18	Roomer	KBB
Hyman, Henry	WM	16	Roomer	KBB
Jaworski, Jos.	WM	18	Roomer	KBB
Jenkins, Gladys	WF	3	Inmate	GHH
John, Henrietta	WF	11	Inmate	GHH
Kachnienciz, Raymond	WM	18	Roomer	KBB
Kato, Hotrunno	WF	27	Boarder	EHG
Katz, Gino	WM	11	-	MBM
Kelly, Wm.	WM	19	Roomer	KBB
Kessler, Henry	WM	18	Roomer	KBB
Ketalainen, Emil	WM	25	Head	HBH
Kctalainen, Mary A.	WF	27	Wife	HBH
Kladek, Walter	WM	10	-	MBM
Koening, Adolph	WM	20	Roomer	KBB
Kronick, Benj.	WM	19	Roomer	KBB
Kuisella, Wm.	WM	16	Roomer	KBB
Lasee, [illegible]	WF	25	Maid	EHG
Launney, Jos.	WM	19	Roomer	KBB
Lawrence, Anthony	WM	18	Roomer	KBB
Leaper, Wesley	WM	21	Roomer	KBB
Lee, Sara	WF	25	Boarder	EHG
Leischner, Rudoph	WM	20	Roomer	KBB
Lenroy, Emma	WF	10	Inmate	GHH
Leonard, Peter J.	WM	18	Boarder	NWS
Loeb, Marie	WF	10	Boarder	EHG
Loeb, Mary	WF	44	Cook	EHG
Logan, Arthur	BM	19	Roomer	KBB
Lopes, Jos.	WM	18	Roomer	KBB
Lovett, Jack	WM	16	Roomer	KBB
Mack, Anna	WF	26	Employee	EHG
Mackowski, Alex	WM	17	Roomer	KBB
Macky, Charlotte	WF	31	Employee	EHG
Maday, Agnes	WF	23	Boarder	EHG
Maguire, Rose	WF	24	Boarder	EHG

Mandoi, Elinore	WF	24	Boarder	EHG
Mankowich, Anna	WF	18	Boarder	EHG
Mannerly, Francis	WM	17	Roomer	KBB
Maoks, Pauline	WF	19	Boarder	EHG
Martin, Anna	WF	37	Wife	MBM
Martin, Inez	WF	24	Boarder	EHG
Martin, John L.	WM	42	Dietitian	MBM
Martinson, Carl G.	WM	18	Roomer	KBB
Maus, Salvatore	WM	18	Roomer	KBB
May, Winifred	WF	28	Boarder	EHG
McArdle, John	WM	10	-	MBM
McNeill, Garfield	W-	41	Staff	GHH
Merrick, Edward	WM	11	-	BMF
Miles, William	WM	6	-	BMF
Miller, Helen	WF	11	Inmate	GHH
Miller, John	WM	16	Roomer	KBB
Mills, Frank	WM	17	Roomer	KBB
Moskovic, Jack	WM	18	Roomer	KBB
Muller, Meyer	WM	18	Roomer	KBB
Murray, Arthur	WM	20	Boarder	NWS
Navy, George	WM	47	Cook	HBH
Neckasian, Samuel	WM	9	-	BMF
Nepucci, Geo.	WM	17	Roomer	KBB
Newman, Morris	WM	18	Caretaker	BMF
Nichols, Chester	BM	18	Roomer	KBB
Nicola, Alfred	WM	18	Boarder	NWS
Noe, Alfonze	BM	17	Roomer	KBB
Noehren, Walter	WM	12	Roomer	KBB
Noel, Grace	WF	23	Boarder	EHG
Nolheru, Walter	WM	12	-	BMF
Nunan, Honor	WF	38	Boarder	EHG
O'Brien, John	WM	17	Roomer	KBB
O'Connor, Philip	WM	23	Roomer	HBH
O'Donnell, Ed.	WM	18	Roomer	KBB
Ogden, Kathryn	W-	25	Cook	GHH
Ogden, Margaret	W-	22	Student	GHH
O'Shea, Teresia	WF	25	Employee	EHG
O'Shea, Tilly M.	WF	60d	-	EHG
Ostroff, David	WM	20	Boarder	NWS
Palmer, Jesse	WM	19	Roomer	KBB
Parker, Charles	WM	19	Roomer	KBB

Pavyale, Jennie	WF	18	Boarder	EHG
Pekar, Jos.	WM	16	Roomer	KBB
Pepper, Henry	WM	17	-	BMF
Perlmutle, Julius	WM	11	-	MBM
Peterson, Caroline E.	W-	41	Superintendant	GHH
Petuchov, Leonard	WM	11	-	BMF
Phillips, Lewis	WM	7	-	BMF
Pierce, Adams	WM	19	Boarder	NWS
Pikary, Lillian	WF	20	Boarder	EHG
Pinatte, Joseph	WM	17	Roomer	KBB
Pism, Ed. R.	WM	18	Roomer	KBB
Pollack, Tillie	WF	17	Boarder	EHG
Prousalons, Polipine	WF	32	Boarder	EHG
Prowse, Arthur	WM	18	Roomer	KBB
Rachin, Ella	WF	19	Boarder	EHG
Ranney, Ernest	WM	61	Boarder	KBB
Raphin, Anita	WF	22	Boarder	EHG
Ravlino, Marie	WF	32	Boarder	EHG
Rietdorf, Ed.	WM	19	Roomer	KBB
Romansky, Wm.	WM	18	Roomer	KBB
Rosenblatt, Morris	WM	15	Roomer	KBB
Russell, Michael	WM	45	Boarder	KBB
Salznan, Harry	W-	21	Night Watchman	GHH
Santamarias, Nicholas	WM	19	Roomer	KBB
Sarapri, Jennie	WF	21	Boarder	EHG
Sassmas, Alex	WM	18	Roomer	KBB
Saunders, Henry	WM	20	-	BMF
Savagi, Marie	WF	25	Boarder	EHG
Saveous, Jean	WF	23	Boarder	EHG
Schipper, Fred	WM	15	-	MBM
Schock, William	WM	15	-	MBM
Schulze, Lydia	WF	19	Boarder	EHG
Schwarz, Emanuel	WM	18	Boarder	NWS
Seidel, Gus	WM	15	Roomer	KBB
Seidel, Wm.	WM	17	Roomer	KBB
Senchock, Jos.	WM	19	Roomer	KBB
Sexton, Rosie	WF	35	Boarder	EHG
Shields, James	WM	17	Roomer	KBB
Slade, Thomas	WM	20	Roomer	KBB
Smith, Frank	WM	10	-	BMF
Smith, Fred	WM	2	-	EHG

Smith, Isadore	WM	14	-	MBM
Snyder, Wm.	BM	17	Roomer	KBB
Sommerfeld, Emma	WF	24	Boarder	EHG
Sonor, Helen	WF	11	Boarder	EHG
Sonor, Marie	WF	41	Employee	EHG
Stanton, John	WM	11	-	MBM
Stephen, Junior	WM	7	-	BMF
Stone, Wm.	WM	66	Boarder	KBB
Stretch, James	WM	11	-	MBM
Szogepanicki, Stanley	WM	18	Roomer	KBB
Taylor, George W.	WM	65	Asst. Super.	NWS
Theise, Beatrice	WF	18	Boarder	EHG
Theise, Esther	WF	21	Boarder	EHG
Thompson, Ervin	WM	19	Roomer	KBB
Traiges, Adolph	WM	18	Roomer	KBB
Tranz, Sophie	WF	15	Inmate	GHH
Treatchek, George	WM	18	Boarder	NWS
Turbin, Dulfey	WM	22	Teamster	BMF
Vargeson, Grace	WF	12	Inmate	GHH
Ward, Edward	WM	10	-	BMF
Ward, John	WM	17	Roomer	KBB
Ward, Leslie	WM	12	-	BMF
Weaver, Howard	WM	16	-	BMF
Wichson, William	BM	8	-	BMF
Williams, Augustus	WM	40	Welfare Worker	NWS
Williams, Frank	WM	18	Roomer	KBB
Williams, Willie	BM	18	Roomer	KBB
Willitt, Anne F.	WF	75	Clerk	EHG
Wood, George	WM	8	-	BMF
Wood, Lulu	W-	15	Caretaker	GHH
Wood, Pearl	W-	45	Camp Advisor	GHH
Yomunas, Amelia	WF	23	Boarder	EHG
Young, Maria	WF	34	Boarder	EHG
Zelder, Cornelia	WF	36	Employee	EHG
Zelder, Edith	WF	2	-	EHG
Zeronicky, Theodore	WM	14	-	BMF
Zidek, John	WM	18	Roomer	KBB

Lodging Houses Omitted from the Index

The following lodging houses of the Children's Aid Society were not included in this index because the residence was not enumerated, the record could not be located, or the record was illegible:

1855	Girls' Lodging House	22 Oliver Street
1860	Girls' Lodging House	181 Cherry Street
1870	Rivington Street Lodging House	325 Rivington Street
	Eleventh Ward Lodging House	709 East 11th Street
1890	West Side Lodging House	400 Seventh Avenue
1910	Temporary Home for Younger Children	442 West 23rd Street
1915	A. Louise Erlanger Home	141 West 61st Street
1920	Kip's Bay Boys' House	825 Second Avenue
1925	A. Louise Erlanger Home	154 East 45th Street

BIBLIOGRAPHY

Brace, Charles Loring. "Address on Industrial Schools." Wynkoop & Hallenbeck, New York. 1868.

Brace, Charles Loring. "The Best Method of Disposing of our Pauper and Vagrant Children." Wynkoop, Hallenbeck & Thomas, New York. 1859.

Brace, Charles Loring. "Children's Lodging Houses." *The New York Times*. November 20, 1868. Page 3, Column 3.

Brace, Charles Loring, 2nd. "Keeping Families Together." *The New York Times*. Section 1, Page 22, Column 7.

Brooklyn Eagle, The. "Saw the Newsboys' Home." February 13, 1901. Page 10, Column 2.

Children's Aid Society, The. "Annual Reports." New York. 1854 to 1925.

Gray, Christopher. "The Tompkin's Square Boys' Lodging House." *The New York Times*. March 31, 1991. Section 10, Page 7, Column 1.

Letchworth, William Pryor. "The History of Child-Saving Work in the State of New York." Press of George Ellis, Boston. June 1893. Pages 22-23.

New York Herald, The. "Mother Explains "Abandonment of Girl with Doll." August 19, 1917. Page 7, Column 6.

New York Sun, The. "Children's Aid Society Give Encouraging News to Parents." December 2, 1925. Page 34.

New York Times, The. "A Day in a Newsboy's Life." July 6, 1890. Page 16, Column 5.

New York Times, The. "Charities in War-Time." March 16, 1865. Page 6, Column 5.

New York Times, The. "Our City Charities." April 7, 1860. Page 2, Column 5.

New York Times, The. "Urchins of the Street." December 19, 1880. Page 2, Column 5.

Poore, C.G. "Story of a Crusade for the City Children." *The New York Times*. April 19, 1928. Section 10, Page 20, Column 1.

www.ingramcontent.com/pod-product-compliance
Lightning Source LLC
Chambersburg PA
CBHW061743270326
41928CB00011B/2349
* 9 7 8 0 8 0 6 3 4 6 2 3 6 *